WALTER SINNOTT-ARMSTRONG

Think Again
How to Reason and Argue

A PELICAN BOOK

PELICAN
an imprint of
PENGUIN BOOKS

PELICAN BOOKS

UK | USA | Canada | Ireland | Australia
India | New Zealand | South Africa

Penguin Books is part of the Penguin Random House
group of companies whose addresses can be found at
global.penguinrandomhouse.com.

Penguin
Random House
UK

First published 2018
003

Text copyright © Walter Sinnott-Armstrong, 2018

The moral right of the author has been asserted

Book design by Matthew Young
Set in 10/14.664 pt FreightText Pro
Typeset by Jouve (UK), Milton Keynes
Printed and bound in Great Britain by Clays Ltd, Elcograf S.p.A.

A CIP catalogue record for this book is
available from the British Library

ISBN: 978-0-141-98311-0

MIX
Paper from
responsible sources
FSC® C018179

In gratitude to Stacey Meyers, Lisa Olds,
Diane Masters, Dana Hall and all of the unsung
heroines who enable me to do what I want.

Contents

ACKNOWLEDGEMENTS

I am grateful to everyone who has argued with me over many years. I have learned from you all. I learned the most from Robert Fogelin – I could not have asked for a more inspiring mentor, collaborator and friend. I also thank Addison Merryman for research assistance, and my editors – Casiana Ionita at Penguin Press and Peter Ohlin at Oxford University Press – for their encouragement and detailed suggestions. I benefited from discussions of these topics with Leda Cosmides, Molly Crockett, Alexa Dietrich, Mike Gazzaniga, Shanto Iyengar, Ron Kassimir, Michael Lynch, Diana Mutz, Nate Persily, Liz Phelps, Steve Sloman, John Tooby and Rene Weber. For helpful comments on the manuscript, I thank Aaron Ancell, Alice Armstrong, Esko Brummel, Jordy Carpenter, Kyra Exterovich-Rubin, Rose Graves, Sandra Luksic, J. J. Moncus, Hannah Read, Sarah Sculco, Gus Skorburg, Valerie Soon, Jesse Summers and Simone Tang.

This book project received generous financial support from Bass Connections at Duke University, the Social Science Research Council, and a subaward agreement from the University of Connecticut with funds provided by Grant

No. 58942 from John Templeton Foundation. Its contents are solely the responsibility of the author and do not necessarily represent the official views of UConn, the John Templeton Foundation, or any funder.

PREFACE: WHY I WROTE THIS BOOK

I have taught courses on reason and argument for over thirty-five years at Dartmouth College and now Duke University. Many students tell me that my courses have helped them in various areas of their lives. They motivate me to keep going.

While my students learned to argue, the rest of the world lost that skill. The level of discourse and communication in politics and also in personal life has reached new lows. During election years, my course has always discussed examples of arguments during presidential debates. During the 1980s, I had no trouble finding arguments on both sides in the debates. Today all I find are slogans, assertions, jokes and gibes, but very few real arguments. I see dismissals, put-downs, abuse, accusations and avoidance of the issue more than actual engagement with problems that matter. There might be fewer protests in the streets today than in the 1960s, but there are still few serious attempts to reason together and understand each other.

I could not help but conclude that our culture, like my students, could benefit from a strong dose of reason and argument. When I moved to Duke in 2010, I was offered a chance to reach a wider audience through the magical medium of MOOCs (that is, Massive Open Online Courses). With my friend Ram Neta I taught a MOOC (*Think Again* on the Coursera platform) that has attracted over 800,000 registered students from over 150 countries. This surprising response convinced me of a hunger around the world for learning how to reason and argue. Of course, not all of my students finished the course, much less learned how to argue well – but many did. My hope is that their new skills helped them understand and work together with their neighbours.

The book that you have in your hands (or on your screen?) is another step in that direction. My goal is to show what arguments are and what good they can do. This book is not about winning arguments or beating opponents. Instead, it is about understanding each other and appreciating strong evidence. It teaches logic instead of rhetorical tricks.

Although this book started as a manual on how to argue, I realized that I also needed to start by explaining why people should argue. That motivational discussion then grew into Part One: Why Argue? The lessons on how to argue then became Part Two, complemented by an overview of how not to argue in Part Three. By the end of the book, I hope that you will be both willing and able to argue and assess arguments as well as to provide motivation and a model for others to join you in constructive engagement. These skills can improve not only your life but also our shared society.

Our Cultural Rut

Calamities threaten our world. War is constant. Terrorism is common. Migrants seek refuge. Poverty is extreme. Inequality is growing. Racial tensions are rising. Women are mistreated. Climate change is looming. Diseases are running rampant. Health costs are soaring. Schools are deteriorating. The news leaves us overwhelmed and depressed.

These crises are gigantic in scope and scale. Because of their immensity, none of these problems can be solved without widespread cooperation. Indeed, real solutions require collaboration among diverse groups of people with conflicting beliefs and values. It's not just that warmongers need to stop fighting, racists need to stop discriminating and ignorant fools need to learn basic facts. In addition, those of us who are neither warmongers nor racists nor fools need to work together despite our differences and disagreements. The refugee problem cannot be solved unless a number of countries with disparate goals and assumptions agree on the nature of the problem and its solution and then come together to convince everyone to do their share. The problem of climate change cannot be solved unless countries all over the world agree that there is a problem and then curtail their production of greenhouse gases. Terrorism cannot be exterminated until every nation denies terrorists safe haven. It will never be enough for one person or even one country to decide what to do and then do it alone. They also need to convince many others to go along.

That much is obvious. What is not so obvious is why smart and caring people do not just do it. Why don't they work together to solve their common problems? Contemporary science gives us remarkable powers to learn, to communicate and to control our futures. Yet we fail to use these abilities for good. So little gets done when so much is at stake! These same problems are bad for those on both sides of the disputes, even if some unfortunate groups are harmed much more than others. And yet politicians from various countries, and indeed politicians within the same country, quibble instead of cooperating, undermine instead of supporting, interrupt instead of listening, and draw lines in the sand instead of proposing compromises that could gain mutual agreement. Politicians add to the problems instead of solving them – or they propose solutions that they know will be rejected immediately by their opponents. Some exceptions – notably the Paris Agreement on climate change – show how countries could work together, but such cooperation is all too rare.

This is not only the case in politics: Facebook, Skype, Snapchat, smartphones and the internet make it much easier than ever before to communicate around the globe, and many people do spend a lot of time talking with friends. Nonetheless, these exchanges almost always occur within bubbles of allies with similar world views. Moreover, discourse has reached a new low on the internet. Complex issues are reduced to 280-character tweets or shorter hashtags and slogans. Even thoughtful tweets and blog posts are often greeted with contempt, gibes, humour and abuse by internet trolls. Moderate opinions encounter immoderate insults that masquerade as wit and spread wilful misinterpretation of opponents. The web makes it easier for large numbers of critics to attack quickly, viciously and thoughtlessly. This new medium and culture reward bluster instead of modesty and leave little incentive to be caring or careful, fair or factual, trustworthy or thoughtful. Rhetoric gains likes. Reason receives dislikes. The medium that should be our tool shapes our actions and goals.

This dark picture is not always accurate, of course, but it is accurate too often. And many of these disparate problems stem largely from the same source: a lack of mutual understanding. Sometimes people avoid talking with each other. Even when they do talk, there is little communication of ideas on important issues. As a result, they cannot figure out why other people believe what they say. Politicians cannot work together, at least partly because they do not understand each other. Opponents will never agree to bear their share of the burden if they do not understand why that burden needs to be carried.

This lack of understanding might sometimes result from incommensurable world views or conflicting assumptions that prevent mutual comprehension. However, political opponents too often do not even *try* to understand each other, partly because they see no personal or political gain in reaching out and being fair. Indeed, they often have strong incentives neither to reach out nor to be fair. Tweeters and bloggers go wild on the internet, because their goal is to gain likes for their jokes and gibes. They receive few such rewards on the internet from balanced attempts to see the other side in contentious debates. Why should they try to understand their opponents when they think that they are bound to fail and get nothing in return for their attempts? Admittedly, many interesting and insightful conversations do occur on Twitter and the internet, but the huge number of lurking trolls scares off many potential contributors.

When they give up on understanding, they turn to wilful misunderstanding and misinterpretation. People on both sides of divisive disputes repeatedly put words into each other's mouths and then retort or snort, 'I cannot imagine why they think that.' Of course they cannot imagine why their rivals think that, because they have formulated their rivals' views in that way precisely in order to make those views look silly. They know or should know that they are misrepresenting their opponents, but they do not care. Their goals are not to convince opponents or to appreciate their positions. They seek only to amuse their allies by abusing their opponents.

These attitudes undermine respect, connection and cooperation. You hold your position; I hold mine. I cannot comprehend how you could be so blind; you have no idea why I am so stubborn. I do not respect your views; you return the favour. We abuse and come to despise each other. I do not want to meet with you; you do not want to deal with me. I refuse to compromise; so do you. Neither of us is open to any possibility of cooperation. No progress is made.

How did we get here?

How did we fall into this cultural hole? How can we climb out? The full story is complex, of course. Anything as wide-spread and intricate as a culture is bound to have many aspects and influences. These issues should not be oversimplified, but it would be overwhelming to try to discuss all of the complications at once. Consequently, this short book will emphasize and explore only one part of the problem. I focus on this one part because it is often overlooked, because it is fundamental, because it lies within my expertise, and because each of us can do something about it in our personal lives instead of having to wait for politicians and cultural leaders to act. We can all start to work on the problem right now.

My answer is that many people have stopped giving reasons of their own and looking for reasons for opposing positions. Even when they give and are given reasons, they do so in a biased and uncritical way, so they fail to understand the reasons on each side of the issue. These people claim too often that their stance is so obvious that anyone who knows what they are talking about will agree with them. If so, opponents must not know what they are talking about. Even before their opponents start talking, these people feel confident that those on the opposing side must all be deeply confused or misinformed or even crazy. They disparage their opponents as so silly that they cannot have any reason at all on their side. Then they cynically assume that reasoning won't do any good anyway, because their opponents are driven only by emotions – fear, anger, hatred, greed or blind compassion – and do not care about truth or about the same values that matter to them. As a result, elections are decided by who gets out the most voters and perhaps by who creates the most rousing or humorous advertisements and slogans instead of by who gives the strongest reasons for their policies. This strategy cannot help us climb out of our rut.

We need to state and understand arguments on both sides. We need to offer our reasons to our opponents and demand reasons from them. Without exchanging reasons, we cannot understand each other. Without understanding, we cannot figure out how to work towards a compromise or cooperation with each other. Without cooperation, we cannot solve our problems. Without solving our problems, we will all be worse off.

How do we get out of here?

This analysis of the problem suggests a solution. We all need to communicate more and in better ways. One crucial step is to assert less and question more. The most useful questions ask why we believe what we do and how our proposals would work. These questions ask for reasons of different kinds (as we will see), so the point is that we need to learn how to ask each other for reasons. Even so, questions are not enough by themselves. Asking for reasons won't help if nobody can supply them. Answers take the form of arguments that express our reasons. Thus we need to learn how to offer appropriate arguments when asked, how to appreciate the arguments that others make, and how to spot weaknesses in our own arguments as well as arguments on the other side. I will try to begin to teach some of these lessons in the following pages.

These lessons need to begin with a rough understanding of what reasons and arguments are. Chapter 6 will go into more detail, but we should head off some common misunderstandings from the start. Many people mistake reasons and arguments for weapons in a war – or at least in a competition, like a debate. That is far from what I am recommending here. Wars and competitions cannot help us work together.

Instead, I will present reasons and arguments as attempts to increase understanding. When I give you a reason to justify my claim, my reason helps you understand why I believe that my claim is true. Similarly, when you give me a reason for your claim, that reason helps me understand why you believe in your claim. Our reasons can achieve these goals without convincing either of us to change our minds at all. We might continue to disagree, but at least we understand each other better. That mutual understanding is what helps us work together.

The same goal can be aided by another kind of reason that explains why something happens. It is useful to know that an event, such as an eclipse, will occur. This knowledge enables you to go and watch the eclipse. However, it does not help you predict future eclipses. You cannot figure out when an eclipse will occur without understanding why eclipses occur (and without a lot more information as well). To predict the future, we need explanations or explanatory reasons why events occur in the present. And we need to be able to predict the future in order to determine which proposal will (in the future) succeed in solving a problem. That is why we need explanatory reasons if we are to work together fruitfully.

Because we need reasons, we also need arguments. The

kind of arguments that I will discuss here are not verbal fights, such as when married couples or political rivals 'argue' by yelling at each other. Arguments as I will present them here are more constructive than that. Roughly, an argument is given when – and only when – someone (the arguer) presents one claim (the premise) as a reason of some kind for another claim (the conclusion). The reason is the premise, and the argument presents that premise as a reason. The purpose of the argument is to express the reason to an audience and thereby to increase their understanding either of why the conclusion is true or why the arguer believes the conclusion.

This definition excludes some exchanges that are often called arguments (such as cursing at another person), and it includes other things that are often not seen as arguments (such as explanations). It does not pretend to capture common usage. Nonetheless, it picks out what we need in order to understand each other and work together.

Although we need more arguments of this kind, we should not argue all day long. Everybody needs a break. Moreover, arguments are not all we need. Arguments do little good when the audience is not receptive, so we also need to learn social skills and habits in order to encourage our audiences to be receptive to reasons. We need to learn modesty (or not claiming to possess the whole truth), graciousness (including conceding opponents' good points), patience (in waiting for audiences to think through our points), and forgiveness (when an opponent refuses to concede our own good points). Although much more is needed, arguments play an important role in a larger scheme that can solve or at least reduce some problems in our culture. Thus arguments are necessary even if they are not sufficient by themselves to solve our problems.

Reason and argument are often presented as if they were enemies of emotion, but that is another misunderstanding to avoid. Reasoning often guides emotions, such as when evidence of a friend's treachery makes me angry at that friend. Indeed, emotions can *be* reasons in the broad sense that I am using here. The premise that I feel love when I am with someone is a *reason* to spend time with my beloved and to believe that this time will be well spent. The premise that I feel fear when I drive too fast is a *reason* not to drive so fast and to believe that driving very fast is dangerous. In such cases, emotions and reasons do not compete and might not even be distinct. Strong feelings can be rational too. We do not always need to suppress emotion and to remain calm in order to use reason and argument.

More generally, misunderstanding reasons and arguments can lead to cynicism and contempt for reasoning and argument. That cynicism and contempt is part of what causes the problem of polarization. Hence, learning to understand and appreciate reasons and arguments properly can help to solve part of the problem. It can help us climb out of our cultural rut.

PART ONE

Why Argue?

So Close and Yet So Far

How many of your close friends hold political views that are diametrically opposed to your own? In other words, if you are liberal, how many of your close friends are very conservative? If you are conservative, how many of your close friends are extremely liberal? And if you are moderate or independent, how many of your close friends hold immoderate positions on either side of the political spectrum? For most people today, the answer is, 'Not many.'

In order to figure out why, we need to ask a few more questions. Would you worry if your child or sibling held a political position diametrically opposed to your own? Would it bother you if they married someone with opposing political views? Would you be scared or annoyed if you had to move into a community where most people vote for a different candidate from the one you vote for? Do you go out of your way to listen to people who disagree with you about politics? Do you read, watch or listen carefully to news that comes from sources that support political positions hostile to your own? Do you despise the party that competes with yours? Do you think that it is a threat to the well-being of your country and of people whom you care about? Do you understand why its supporters prefer it and its candidates?

Do you recognize any good reasons for their positions? Can you explain fairly why they take the stands they do on crucial issues? How sure are you that you are right about the political issues that divide you from them?

In many countries around the world, these questions receive different answers today from those they received only a decade or two ago. Today many people have few close friends with radically different political views, live in communities with vast majorities that support the same political party, read or listen to news sources that agree with them, build social media networks with only political allies, and rarely come across people who express views hostile to their own. When they do encounter such views, they almost never talk at length or try very hard to understand why those people disagree so much with them. When they talk with opponents, they do not try to give reasons, but instead resort to emotional appeals, verbal abuse, jokes at their expense and threats of ostracism or worse. Or they quickly change the subject in order to avoid uncomfortable disagreements. None of these reactions builds bridges or solves problems.

Sceptics might wonder, however, whether we really are as polarized and isolated as I have been suggesting. After all, many people hold moderate or mixed political views, even if they do not usually express them loudly or go into politics. Most of us do know some people with opposing political views, even if we usually avoid talking with them about politics. Opposing political parties do hold lengthy debates in most democracies, even if those debaters often sidestep the real issues. Parties write platforms, even if they rarely follow them. Politicians do support their positions in various news media, even if only by reasserting them. Such exchanges often seem to give reasons for each side's views. And both sides tend to think that they understand their opponents perfectly well. Sometimes political opponents even like each other. So maybe the 'culture wars' are exaggerated.

In order to determine the depth and breadth of polarization, this chapter will consider some empirical research on polarization. A boatload has been written on this topic, so we can only survey a small sample, but we can still learn a lot from this research, starting with the United States and then turning to other countries.

What is polarization?

Polarization is hard to study, partly because it means different things to different people.[1] Sometimes polarization is measured in this way:

> *Distance*: groups are more distant from each other when their views are further apart on some relevant scale.

Of course, there can be a great distance between the average views of two groups even when there is also a large area of overlap between these groups – if the individuals in these groups vary enough among themselves. Imagine a scale of left (liberal) to right (conservative) orientation in politics from 0 to 10. If a liberal party varies from 0 to 7 with an average of 3 and a conservative party varies from 3 to 10 with an average of 7, then a lot of people between 3 and 7 will share views, even though they are in competing parties whose averages lie far apart.

For this reason, some researchers and commentators usually add another measure of polarization:

Homogeneity: groups are more internally homogeneous when there is less variance among members of each group.

Distance plus homogeneity equals polarization. These features combined are enough to capture the metaphor of 'poles apart', since the North and South Poles are a great distance from each other.

Still, merely being far apart does not ensure that parties and people will not get along. For one thing, we might disagree a lot about issues that do not matter much to us. Many Taiwanese like stinky tofu, and I love it, but many Americans find it disgusting. These views on stinky tofu are extremely different, but that kind of polarization does not create any serious problems. Neither group dislikes the other because of its views on stinky tofu. They just eat what they want.

Conflicts do not arise until we add more to distance plus homogeneity:

Antagonism: groups are more polarized when they feel more hatred, disdain, fear, or other negative emotions towards people at the other pole.

Antagonism is about how people feel, but these private feelings often get expressed in public speech:

Incivility: groups are more polarized when they talk more negatively about the people at the other pole.

Negative speech causes feelings of hatred, and this hatred leads people to use more negative epithets, which leads to more hatred, which leads to more epithets, and so on. Antagonism and incivility reinforce each other in a vicious circle.

Bad feelings and bad speech are bad enough, but what matters more are actions. In order to move beyond feelings and speech to actions, many commentators also associate polarization with certain barriers in political or private life:

Rigidity: groups are more polarized to the extent that they treat their values as sacred rights on which they refuse to compromise.

Rigidity is clearly connected to the intensity of one's emotions and values as well as one's views of the source of those values. Because cooperation often requires compromise, rigidity can lead to:

Gridlock: groups are more polarized to the extent that they are unable to cooperate and work together towards common goals.

Gridlock is often what bothers people most about polarization, because it prevents government actions that can solve social problems.

Governments can still function when society is split between groups that are polarized, antagonistic and rigid if one group has all or most of the power, either because it constitutes a significant majority or because it has somehow grabbed the reins of government. Thus gridlock in the sense of inability to get anything done occurs only if neither group can lord it over the other. Still, even if one group dominates and gets what it wants, gridlock in the sense of groups being unable to work together is undesirable as long as both groups should have some control over the institutions that govern them.

Gridlock also might seem less likely or less dangerous in governments with more than two parties, such as those in Germany, Israel, India, the United Kingdom, and many other countries. In such systems, different parties need to work together in order to form coalitions that achieve a majority. Nonetheless, such coalitions can still easily become antagonistic, rigid and incapable of working with anyone outside of the ruling coalition. Then there is polarization between coalitions instead of between single parties, but the same problems can arise.

So, what is polarization? All of the above. The full syndrome includes every one of these aspects – distance, homogeneity, antagonism, incivility, rigidity, gridlock – and more. This complexity cannot be simplified without distorting the issue. Still, when we discuss polarization, we should not talk about all of these aspects at once. In order to avoid confusion, we need to know which specific features of polarization are relevant to each particular discussion.

Are the poles moving apart?

How much polarization exists? Let's start by looking at polarization understood simply as distance plus homogeneity. How can we measure distance and homogeneity? In politics, the standard method is to ask randomly selected members of a group to respond to a variety of statements (with typical liberal and conservative responses). Distance between the groups is measured by how far apart the average answers for each group are. Homogeneity within a group is measured by how close the answers of different members of the group are. We can use these questionnaires to track trends in this kind of polarization over time.

In the United States, polarization seems to have grown tremendously in the decades since the 1990s. That impression is widespread and supported by surveys. First consider distance between the parties, called the partisan gap. This gap has increased over a wide variety of issues. Here are some dramatic examples:[2]

'The best way to ensure peace is through military strength.'
— 1994: 44 per cent of Republicans and 28 per cent of
   Democrats agreed.
— 2014: 48 per cent of Republicans and 18 per cent of
   Democrats agreed.
On this issue, the partisan gap almost doubled from 16 per cent to 30 per cent.

'Government regulation of business usually does more harm than good.'
— 1994: 64 per cent of Republicans and 46 per cent of
   Democrats agreed.
— 2014: 68 per cent of Republicans and 29 per cent of
   Democrats agreed.
On this issue, the partisan gap more than doubled from 18 per cent to 39 per cent.

'Stricter environmental laws and regulations cost too many jobs and hurt the economy.'
— 1994: 39 per cent of Republicans and 29 per cent of
   Democrats agreed.

— 2014: 59 per cent of Republicans and 24 per cent of Democrats agreed.

On this issue, the partisan gap more than tripled from 10 per cent to 35 per cent.

'Poor people today have it easy because they can get government benefits without doing anything in return.'
— 1994: 63 per cent of Republicans and 44 per cent of Democrats agreed.
— 2014: 66 per cent of Republicans and 28 per cent of Democrats agreed.

On this issue, the partisan gap doubled from 19 per cent to 38 per cent.

'Blacks who can't get ahead in this country are mostly responsible for their own condition.'
— 1994: 66 per cent of Republicans and 53 per cent of Democrats agreed.
— 2014: 79 per cent of Republicans and 50 per cent of Democrats agreed.

On this issue, the partisan gap more than doubled from 13 per cent to 29 per cent.

Notice that Republicans changed more on some issues, whereas Democrats changed more on others. Each side often blames their opponent for creating polarization by moving to an extreme position, but actually both sides have moved, though to different degrees on different issues. The result is that the gap between Republicans and Democrats has increased significantly in a short time on many central issues.[3]

Can't we at least agree on the facts?

These studies focus on political values and norms, but polarization also extends to religion and even to matters of fact. Democrats and Republicans disagree strongly about whether climate change is caused or exacerbated by human greenhouse gas emissions. That is a scientific issue that could potentially be settled independently of whether one thinks that greenhouse gas emissions and climate change are bad, good or neutral. Despite this possibility, politics often drives scientific beliefs instead of science driving policy. Similarly, Democrats and Republicans have very divergent factual beliefs about other factual issues, including these:

1. whether fracking is dangerous
2. whether capital punishment deters murder
3. whether waterboarding is effective in fighting terrorism
4. whether gun ownership promotes or reduces gun violence
5. whether social welfare programmes help or hurt economic growth
6. how many immigrants entered the United States illegally
7. how many illegal immigrants are criminals
8. how many illegal immigrants take jobs that citizens want
9. how much voter fraud is committed in United States elections
10. whether there were weapons of mass destruction in Iraq before the United States attacked

Most Democrats give different answers to these questions than most Republicans, suggesting that these parties cannot agree on facts any more than they can on values.

Liberals sometimes blame conservatives for this problem because they think that conservatives base their factual beliefs on religious or other unreliable authorities instead of on science. At the same time it is worth noting that liberals often reject the scientific consensus on whether genetically modified foods are safe, whether vaccinations cause autism, or whether nuclear wastes can be disposed of safely.[4] On the other hand, Republicans are more likely to reject the scientific consensus on climate change, though conservatives who doubt man-made climate change do not show less scientific literacy.[5] Thus neither side has a monopoly on scientific evidence or on the facts.

Facts and values are connected, of course. If we do not agree whether capital punishment deters or whether global warming is caused by human activity, then it should come as no surprise when we also disagree about whether to allow capital punishment or to fight global warming. When people do not agree on crucial facts, they are unlikely to agree about what to do in face of the facts.

Given such widespread disagreement, it is surprising how confident both sides are. Many defenders of capital punishment are completely sure that it is a deterrent, while many opponents of capital punishment have little doubt that it does not deter. One explanation might be that they have never seen data that support the other side, perhaps because they have never looked for data on the other side of the dispute or have never consulted sources that were likely to contain such data. Whatever the explanation, their confidence is astonishing – given the difficulty of the issues, the presence of conflicting data and arguments, and the lack of consensus.

Do you hate your opponents?

The problem is not only that people hold strongly opposing views with such confidence. I am a philosopher, so some of my closest colleagues think that my philosophical views are necessarily false – that my claims could not possibly be true. They hold philosophical views that are as strongly opposed to mine as any view could be. They also hold their own opinions with great confidence. Nonetheless, we can still be friends. They do not think that I am stupid, dangerous or immoral – I hope – just because I take certain stands that are mistaken in their opinion. They listen carefully to me as I develop my positions, and they try their best to understand my perspective. They do not engage in verbal abuse or vicious jokes that distort my views for their fun at my expense. Instead, they give their arguments and think carefully about how I would or could best reply. At least many of them do. When opponents remain civil, we can learn from each other and stay friends.

Polarization understood simply as distance and homogeneity is not the fundamental problem. Indeed, a different problem would arise if there were too little distance between the parties. Previous generations sometimes complained that the Republican and Democratic parties in the United States were so similar that voters did not have any significant choice between policy alternatives.[6] Moreover, polarization understood as distance and homogeneity has not always led to intense conflict and gridlock, even when the presidency and Congress were divided between parties.[7]

Two people who hold views at opposite ends of the political spectrum might still be able to cooperate if they share enough common goals, are humble enough to admit that they do not know the whole truth, and like each other enough to listen to each other, understand each other and work towards mutually beneficial agreements. In contrast, they won't be able to accomplish anything if they despise each other, refuse to listen, are too over-confident, and lose all willingness or ability to reach a compromise. What creates the practical problem, then, is not simply polarization understood as distance plus homogeneity, but, instead, antagonism and the resultant inability to move past roadblocks.

Unfortunately, increasing polarization in the United States does engender more and more hatred – or at least antagonism – between the major political parties.[8] In 1994, only 16 per cent of Democrats and 17 per cent of Republicans held a very unfavourable view of the other party. By 2016, majorities in both parties expressed very unfavourable views of the other party: 58 per cent of Republicans and 55 per cent of Democrats.

Even more alarmingly, 45 per cent of Republicans in 2016 saw policies of the Democratic Party as 'so misguided that they threaten the nation's well-being', and 41 per cent of Democrats in 2016 felt the same about Republican Party policies. These percentages are much higher among consistently conservative Republicans and consistently liberal Democrats.

Those who care about their country will fight what they see as threats to their country's well-being, so they will have little or no incentive to work and live together with people whom they see as dangerous.

This antipathy exists not just between parties and politicians. It extends into personal life. In 2010, 49 per cent of Republicans and 33 per cent of Democrats in the United States reported that they would be displeased if their child married outside of their political party, whereas less than 5 per cent of both parties had said this in 1960.[9] Polarized politics has even infected personal relations.

It also affects where Americans live. In 2014, 50 per cent of consistently conservative Republicans and 35 per cent of consistently liberal Democrats agreed with the statement, 'It is important to me to live in a place where most people share my political views.'[10] As a result, consistent conservatives and consistent liberals often end up living in different locations, so that they do not run into each other as often as they would if they lived next door. Similarly, 63 per cent of consistently conservative Republicans and 49 per cent of consistently liberal Democrats agreed that 'Most of my close friends share my political views.' None of these figures was nearly as high twenty years earlier. This geographical and social segregation makes it hard to see how these groups can ever start talking with each other or overcome their mutual antagonism.

Has the epidemic gone global?

So far, my statistics and examples have focused on the United States, but the same problems exist elsewhere. Polarization runs rampant in many other countries throughout the world. Surprisingly, 'On average, Americans view their parties as much further apart than voters in other countries.'[11] However, the reverse is actually true: 'On the economic dimension, the distance between Democrats and Republicans is not especially large, relative to other countries. On the social dimension, the distance is quite small in comparative perspective.'[12] Of course, even if distance between political parties is greater in other countries than in the United States, other aspects of polarization, such as gridlock, might be worse in the United States than in those other countries, partly because of the many checks and balances written into the United States Constitution. Nonetheless, many examples show that distance between, coherence within, hatred of, and lack of reasoning between political parties is at least as fierce in other countries.

One example is the recent Brexit vote in the United Kingdom, which revealed deep and widespread social and ideological divisions. The recent migrant crisis has also produced extreme antagonism between left and right on the European continent. This unfortunate trend is not confined to Europe. Political polarization in Sri Lanka has led to outrageous hate speech on both sides.[13] Polarization in Thailand has led to massive protests.[14] Interestingly, South Korea and Taiwan exhibit high levels of affective polarization – antagonism towards political opponents – despite low levels of ideological polarization.[15] Why would people within a country dislike each other so much when their political views are not very far apart? I cannot help but suspect that part of the cause is refusal to listen to the other side's reasoning.

This problem is not universal: Iceland might be an exception. There is 'no sign of real polarization in Icelanders' left–right self-placement'.[16] Nonetheless, even in Iceland, 'The media paints a picture of [Iceland's] Parliament as increasingly divided',[17] and the public has a false impression of increasing polarization: 'not only did both liberals and conservatives exaggerate how much the other group would espouse certain stereotypical values (moral values), but they also estimated that their own group would be more extreme on stereotypical traits than it actually was'.[18] Cases like Iceland must make one wonder whether polarization in other countries is really as bad as it seems.

But even the impression of polarization can lead to antagonism and undermine understanding, empathy and cooperation. If I think that you hold an extreme view that is diametrically opposed to my own, and if I think that anyone who disagrees with me must be either ignorant or immoral, then those assumptions together can be enough to make me despise and avoid you. It can surely make it hard for us to understand each other and to talk, reason and work together. The impression of polarization is a kind or source of polarization – or at least it is almost as harmful.

CHAPTER 2

Toxic Talk

Why have we moved so far apart and become so antagonistic? These cultural phenomena are massively complex. No single explanation can do justice to all of the many influences that push opponents apart. Still, we can learn a lot by focusing on one factor which is often overlooked. Here it is: instead of listening to and trying to understand our opponents, we interrupt, caricature, abuse and joke about them and their views. This toxic way of talking exemplifies the aspect of polarization that I labelled 'incivility'.

Can we be civil, please?

Like 'polarization', the term 'civility' is used in several different ways. Moreover, civility and incivility are in the eye (or the ear) of the beholder. One person's spirited criticism is another person's incivility. Civility also comes in degrees. Some words and actions are more or less polite than others. Despite these complications, civility can be understood as a vague ideal that we can approach more or less closely. Incivility is a significant deviation from this ideal.

Speech is civil when people talk in ways that are tailored to bring about a constructive mutual exchange of ideas. An extreme model of civility is suggested by Anatol Rapoport, a mathematical psychologist who was famous for his insights into social interactions:

1. You should attempt to re-express your target's position so clearly, vividly, and fairly that your target says, 'Thanks, I wish I'd thought of putting it that way.'
2. You should list any points of agreement (especially if they are not matters of widespread agreement).
3. You should mention anything that you have learned from your target.
4. Only then are you permitted to say so much as a word of rebuttal or criticism.[1]

How many times have you heard or participated in a conversation that obeys these rules? Such guidelines have gone out of fashion recently, if they were ever followed. Luckily, we do not need to go so far in order to maintain minimal politeness. We can be civil to the degree that we approach this ideal.

That's not all there is to civility, of course. Timing is also important. While you are explaining your view to me, if I interrupt and prevent you from finishing what you were saying, then it won't help much if I express your position clearly, vividly and fairly. You wanted to express it yourself. Interruption is a paradigm of incivility because it sends the signal that I do not want to listen to you, or at least that what you say is less valuable than what I say. Civility, therefore, requires the virtue of patience: we should wait for our audience as they take time to speak their minds. It also requires forgiveness when others refuse to concede our best points.

None of this is easy, but we do have a choice. We can

express civility by following or at least approaching the Rapoport Rules: speaking and listening at the right times without interrupting, and cultivating patience and forgiveness. Or we can practise incivility by interrupting, insulting and abusing our opponents. Your style is up to you.

Who doesn't like a good caricature?

Instead of civilly asking why people adopt their positions, today we tend to assume that we already know their reasons. Of course, the reasons that we ascribe to them are rarely their real reasons, and they are rarely the best reasons for their views. Instead, we too often try to beat opponents by putting them in a bad light.

Consider financial inequality: Poor people accuse the wealthy of greed and demand higher taxes. Rich people accuse poor people of laziness and see taxes as theft by government or, worse, communism. Each side claims to understand the other, but only because they both think that their opponents are out for short-sighted, selfish gain. Poor people ask: What can a super-wealthy person do with an extra billion dollars? Don't they see that the whole country needs extra tax revenue? But then the wealthy respond: Don't they see that I worked hard for my money? Don't they realize that higher taxes will hurt the entire economy, especially the poor? As long as neither side understands the other, they will continue to see their opponents as stupid, misinformed, short-sighted and selfish. That will make cooperation difficult or impossible. Such caricatures are harmful.

They are also inaccurate. Some wealthy people are greedy

and selfish. Others are generous, hard-working and fair to their employees and customers. Similarly, poor people are not generally lazy. Some are. Some unemployed people who live on welfare would not accept a job if you offered them one. However, they are exceptions to the rule that most poverty results from bad circumstances with no options. There is truth on both sides. We need to recognize that complexity and determine which poor people fall into which group – the lazy and the disadvantaged – if we are ever to devise a programme that helps those in real need without rewarding and encouraging those who misuse the system.

The same pattern recurs with the refugee crisis. While visiting Oxford, I heard those who supported the policy of allowing more refugees into the UK asking how their opponents could be so cruel. Didn't they realize how desperate the refugees were? Didn't they know how dangerous their home countries were? In such ways, they suggested that their opponents were ignorant and heartless. In return, the opponents of allowing more refugees into the UK asked how others could be so naive. Didn't they realize how many refugees there were? Didn't they care about British citizens who could lose jobs if more refugees arrived? Didn't they care about security? Did they want to bring more terror attacks to British soil? Thus they also suggested that their opponents were ignorant and heartless. Instead of trying to understand each other, both sides spread inaccurate caricatures of their opponents. Making such assumptions and tossing around such misleading stereotypes make it much harder for them to understand each other properly.

Are we all crazy clowns?

Such (intentional?) misunderstanding fuels exaggeration and verbal abuse. One particularly pernicious form of verbal abuse is fake psychiatric diagnosis. Of course, psychiatric diagnoses can be fine when done properly on the basis of evidence by trained psychiatrists in order to help patients with real mental illnesses. The problem is that political and cultural commentators today diagnose their opponents with no evidence or training, and their goal is not to help them but only to abuse them. Books by conservative commentators have titles like *Liberalism is a Mental Disorder* (Michael Savage), *The Liberal Mind: The Psychological Causes of Political Madness* (Lyle Rossiter) and *Brainwashed: How Universities Indoctrinate America's Youth* (Ben Shapiro). Liberals return the favour with titles like *How the Right Lost its Mind* (Charles J. Sykes). Mika Brzezinski, a liberal news commentator on MSNBC, openly expressed grave concern that President Donald Trump was mentally ill.

To see the purpose and effect of such exaggeration, let's consider some simple examples from the popular conservative commentator Ben Shapiro:

> The democrats are fully extreme. They are fully insane. They are nutcases, they are nuts.

> The democrats are out of their damn minds. They are out of their damn minds.[2]

Why does he call his opponents crazy? It is obvious that not all Democrats are crazy, insane, nutcases or out of their damn minds. So what is the objective of such extreme language? One goal is to get laughs from his audience. It also signals his solidarity with Republicans and hatred for Democrats. What matters here is that it cuts off conversation. When people really are 'fully insane' or 'out of their damn minds', then there is no reason to listen to them. It might be useful for therapists to listen to them in order to find out which mental illness they have, and it might be calming to them for friends and relatives to listen to or talk with them. But that is not really having a conversation in the sense of an intentional exchange of information and reasons. When people are 'fully insane', we do not bother to tell them what is wrong with their views or give them reasons to change. We try to cure them instead of reasoning with or learning from them.

Other forms of verbal abuse impose similar costs. If I tell my friend that her position is wrong, she can ask me why it is wrong, and then we can still have a fruitful discussion in many cases. However, if I tell her that her position is ridiculous, that means that it deserves ridicule instead of reason. If she does not want to be ridiculed, why should she ask me why I think her position is ridiculous? And if I call her a clown, it suggests that her view deserves laughter instead of serious consideration. It ruins a clown's jokes to take them seriously and ask what they really mean. Similarly, if I call my interlocutor an idiot, it means that she is too stupid to deserve any reason. But then, why should she keep talking with me? I just told her that I am not going to listen to her.

Some views really are ridiculous, and some people really are idiots or crazy – though very rarely. Also, sometimes people ask for reasons and try to understand before they resort to verbal abuse out of frustration if their initial attempts have failed. Nonetheless, fake psychiatry of this abusive kind is a reliable indicator that the speaker has nothing better – and hence nothing very insightful – to say in favour of his position. Such verbal abuse also signals the end of fruitful discussion. When polar opposites resort to it, they cease to be able to learn from each other. Nobody gains.

Are insults funny?

Sometimes abuse can be fun and funny. Don Rickles, the famous comedian, developed insult humour into a popular art. Many people today imitate his comedy routines in real life and on the internet. The recent presidential primaries in the US were filled with demeaning jokes by Donald Trump and his followers about 'Little Marco' (Rubio, who was one of Trump's competitors in Republican primaries). After Trump was elected, liberals (and some of Trump's conservative opponents) engaged in silly jests about the size of Trump's hands. Such humour is so juvenile that it is hard to believe that anyone takes it seriously.

What exactly do we gain from a joke at our opponent's expense? Of course, we get pleasure. It feels good to laugh. But that is only the start of an explanation, because we could also get such pleasant feelings from jokes about our own limitations. So why make fun of opponents instead of ourselves?

Maybe such jokes affect voting. Who wants to support a candidate who will be a laughing stock? Still, it is hard to believe that anyone who supports Trump would turn to the other side because of the size of his hands.

The real goal of such jokes, I suspect, is to build group solidarity. Making fun of opponents is rewarded by laughter and praise from like-minded audiences who agree with us. This reaction signals to us all that we share certain values, which motivates us to hang together as a group or as a movement. Joking about a view or opinion also shows that we do not take it seriously, so we are unlikely to be swayed onto that opposing side. That signals our stability, which gives people confidence in cooperating with us. Finally, the ability to make the best joke at an opponent's expense also gains us status as a leader in the group. That is why some members of the group compete to tell the funniest or most vicious jokes at the expense of outsiders.

Jokes about opponents are also particularly effective because they leave those opponents with no good response. If they do not laugh at the jokes about themselves, then they come off as stiffs who lack a sense of humour, arrogantly denying their own flaws, or as too dumb to get the joke. There is no way for them to win.

In these ways, jokes about opponents work as rhetorical tricks. They can build groups, gain status for the joker and rob the target of any way to recover. That explains why humour has become such a common weapon. However, such humour also has a dark side. Joking about someone's position will impede understanding of that position. You cannot appreciate opponents or their reasoning by making them look silly. They are almost never as silly as the jokes make them look. Moreover, if you joke about them, then they will joke about you. Each side replies in kind, so the level of discourse spirals down.

I am not denying that humour has a place. It can lighten the atmosphere and enable good feelings for each other. Intelligent political satire can be insightful political critique when it draws attention to bad arguments and falsehoods. However, simplistic and vicious humour that abuses outsiders rarely accomplishes constructive goals in the long run. Instead, it prevents us from understanding and empathizing with each other.

How low can we go?

Abuse gets more vicious on the internet, perhaps because abusers are anonymous and do not have to face their victims. Sometimes internet trolls go so far as to threaten their targets. There are plenty of examples, but I will focus on one, because I happen to know the victim.

A philosophy professor at Emory College in Atlanta, George Yancy, wrote a controversial piece, 'Dear White America', in *The Stone* (part of *The New York Times*) on 24 December 2015. Yancy's letter starts,

> I have a weighty request. As you read this letter, I want you to listen with love, a sort of love that demands that you look at parts of yourself that might cause pain and terror, as James Baldwin would say. Did you hear that? You may have missed it. I repeat: I want you to listen with love. Well, at least try.

Next, he admits to being sexist himself, and he explains what that means. Then he says,

Just as my comfort in being male is linked to the suffering of women, which makes me sexist, so, too, you are racist.

Yancy knew, of course, that calling his readers racist would produce negative reactions. However, the onslaught that he received was surprisingly vicious.

Immediately after the publication of 'Dear White America', I began to receive vile and vitriolic white racist comments sent to my university email address, and verbal messages sent to my answering machine. I even received snail mail that was filled with hatred. Imagine the time put into actually sitting down and writing a letter filled with so much hate and then sending it snail mail, especially in our world of the internet. The comments were not about pointing out fallacies in my position, but were designed to violate, to leave me psychologically broken and physically distraught. Words do things, especially words like 'nigger', or being called an animal that should go back to Africa or being told that I should be 'beheaded ISIS style'. (*The Stone*, 18 April 2016)

The crucial point made by Yancy here – in the context of our discussion on reasoning and argument – is: 'The comments were not about pointing out fallacies in my position.' As a philosopher, he would be used to accusations of fallacies. He did not object to criticisms backed by arguments, and we can certainly envisage countless objections to calling so many people (all of 'White America'!) racist. But what he received were not only objections but very personal attacks. Such vicious replies to a gentle man who asks you to listen with love are bound to lead to polarization.

Yancy's story is not typical, fortunately. Many people today still communicate in courteous ways. They often talk with opponents, seek opposing points of view, ask questions and learn from the answers, and do not simply caricature, diagnose, abuse, joke and threaten their opponents. We are able to talk honestly and openly, but too often we do not exercise that ability. Instead, we talk in a toxic way – especially on the internet. This toxic talk signals disrespect and contempt, which fuel antagonism and polarization. It also scares away moderate contributors. Some kinds of incivility to others can be amusing and can create bonds among abusers who share a common target. Nonetheless, these short-term benefits bring long-term costs that are tearing our societies apart and preventing us from solving our serious problems.

Is Europe civilized?

Maybe the situation is not so bad in Europe? This hope has been refuted by the recent Brexit vote in the United Kingdom (perhaps soon not to be so united). One of the champions of the movement to leave the European Union was Boris Johnson, the former Mayor of London who went on to become Secretary of State for Foreign and Commonwealth Affairs. Johnson said,

> I believe we would be mad not to take this once in a lifetime chance to walk through that door because the truth is it is not we who have changed. It is the EU that has changed out of all recognition; and to keep insisting that the EU is about economics is like saying the Italian Mafia is interested in olive oil and real estate.[3]

By calling his opponents 'mad', he removes any incentive to listen to their reasons. Madness precludes listening in order to learn. His reference to a 'once in a lifetime chance' then issues a demand: now or never. It also suggests that there cannot be any compromise, since accepting a compromise would miss the only chance and make it impossible ever to leave the European Union again. And, of course, comparing the European Union with the Mafia implies that they are criminals that need to be stopped before they kill or rob the UK. The only way to stop the Mafia is with weapons, not reasoning. In all of these ways, then, Johnson's description the problem is fashioned to stimulate hatred and silence any balanced discussion of the arguments on both sides.

Those who opposed Brexit were no better. They often said or implied that support for Brexit was based only on fear, anger, Islamophobia, xenophobia and/or racism. Fear and anger often block careful reasoning, so the claim that your opponents are driven by such emotions suggests that there is no point in giving them reasons, much less listening to their reasons. The terms 'Islamophobia' and 'xenophobia' suggest mental illness – phobias – so there is no more point in trying to reason with an Islamophobe or a xenophobe than there is in telling an arachnophobe that many spiders are not really dangerous. And racism is defined by regarding or treating races differently when there is no reason to do so. It is not racist to treat people from other racial backgrounds differently when there is good reason for such treatment, for example in testing for sickle-cell anaemia, which is almost exclusively confined to people of African heritage. Thus epithets like 'racist' lead people not to expect any reasonable arguments or any rational responses to reasoned arguments. Such words suggest that we need to fight these opponents instead of listening to them.

Indeed, those who want to allow immigrants into society sometimes seem to suggest that we should kick out their opponents. Baroness Sayeeda Warsi, former co-Chair of the UK Conservative Party, opposed Brexit because 'Toxic, divisive and xenophobic political campaigning should have no place in a liberal democracy.'[4] No place at all? I would have thought that liberal democracies were liberal because they allowed freedom of speech, including xenophobic political campaigning. Warsi might not have meant to say that such campaigning should be illegal or that xenophobes should be banished – but instead that liberal democracies would be better without them. Still, her vague and incendiary language suggests that we have nothing to learn from these opponents. In that way, it seems to contribute to antagonism and prevent constructive exchanges of reasons.

Of course, not everyone resorts to such rhetorical tricks. J. K. Rowling, author of the acclaimed Harry Potter series, tried to carve out a moderate position between the poles:

> It is dishonourable to suggest, as many have, that Leavers [supporters of Brexit] are all racists and bigots: they aren't and it is shameful to suggest that they are. Nevertheless, it is equally nonsensical to pretend that racists and bigots aren't flocking to the 'Leave' cause, or that they aren't, in some instances, directing it.[5]

A nice distinction! Even if most Leavers are not racist, it still might be true that most racists are Leavers and even that 'some' (maybe many, but not all or even most) of the directors of the Brexit movement are racist. However, when reasonable people tried to calm down the rhetoric, they were often dismissed, as in this case:

> [British liberal elites] tried to make a distinction between a rational anti-immigrant sentiment and an irrational racism, the former to be absorbed into the mainstream, the latter to be marginalized. In fact, no such distinction existed and acting as if it did had the effect of further legitimizing racism in the political mainstream.[6]

Replies like this accuse all moderates of 'legitimizing racism'. It is no wonder that many people did not have the courage to express moderate views, for they would be labelled 'racist' by one side and 'mad' by the other.

The recent migrant crisis has also produced extreme reactions on the European continent. Although German Chancellor Angela Merkel is usually firmly centrist, she supported immigration by saying, 'When it comes to human dignity, we cannot make compromises.'[7] This statement implies that she will not talk or listen to anyone who suggests a compromise, even, for example, minimal limits on the number of immigrants. If preventing migration violates human dignity, then limiting migration would be comparable to allowing a little slavery.

On the other side, Marine Le Pen, President of the National Front in France, said, 'They don't tell you this, but the immigration crisis in France is totally out of control. My aim is clear: to stop immigration both legal and illegal.' Thus, like Merkel, Le Pen also demonstrates an unwillingness to compromise. She refuses to accept even limited immigration, because then those immigrants would enter legally, contrary to her aim. Le Pen concludes, 'What is at stake in this election is whether France can still be a free nation. The divide is no longer between the left and right, but between patriots and globalists!'[8] Here she labels her opponents as unpatriotic and enemies of a free France, and her extreme positions were endorsed by over one third of French voters in the 2017 election. Of course, there are also supporters of immigration in France and opponents of immigration in Germany. Nonetheless, political leaders in both countries talk about immigration in divisive ways that suggest a lack of willingness to compromise or even listen to any arguments on the other side. It is no surprise that these opponents move further and further apart, and that their mutual antagonism and disrespect grow.

How much incivility is too much?

Why has incivility spread around the world? Why do so many people talk this way even when what they say is literally false? Part of the answer is that incivility is a useful tool for some purposes.

Incivility attracts attention. People see polite messages as bland and boring, so they read and recommend – as well as tweet and retweet – them less than rude exaggerations.[9] Opponents retweet uncivil outbursts in order to show how silly they are and how important it is to oppose such extremists. Nonetheless, they still pay more attention than if these outbursts had been balanced and reasonable.

Incivility also energizes. Supporters retweet their own side's incivility in order to stir up the troops and build passion and energy on their side. A movement can gather more protesters by calling their opponents 'crazy' than by saying that they have missed a few important points.

Incivility also stimulates memory. It is easier to recall an extreme exaggeration that angers you than a balanced and nuanced description of the facts. To prove this, just try to remember what a politician said in a speech. Most people can probably restate the uncivil portions but not the more courteous and balanced parts of the speech.

In these ways, incivility, exaggeration and extremism increase audiences. If what you want is a big audience, this simple strategy is tempting. As marketing it works – and marketing has its place. Powerless groups in society might have no other way to gain attention. Calls for them to remain civil in effect demand them to defer to authority. Movements on their behalf sometimes – especially at the start – need to use incivility. Abolitionists, suffragettes and civil rights leaders were not always courteous (or even peaceful), and their incivility sometimes served their purposes of building their movements.[10] Many of us have benefited from some incivility in this way.

This strategy has costs, however. The relevant cost here is polarization. When opponents are rude to you, it makes you angry and motivates you to retaliate. When you are uncivil to your opponents, this rarely convinces them and often makes them less willing to listen and less able to understand your position. When both sides engage in incivility, they think less of each other and of each other's ideas.[11]

This polarization harms both sides. More important, it undermines our shared society. The many moderates who really want to understand the issues and the reasons on both sides of an argument are deprived of any rational way to decide what to do, because they cannot learn from uncivil tirades. They lose faith in both sides and in news sources that align with either side. Moreover, our government becomes less able to function. Why should I work with someone who calls me stupid and crazy? How could I compromise with such disrespectful opponents?

Because incivility has both costs and benefits, it is often hard to tell when it is justified overall. Insults and sarcasm are bound to remain popular for those who see their benefits as greater than their costs. Meanwhile, the rest of us will suffer.

CHAPTER 3

The Sound
of Silencing

How does incivility fuel polarization? Partly by increasing antagonism, but also by silencing reasoning in ways that prevent us from overcoming our antagonisms. There is more to the story, of course, but this chapter will focus on the part of the story that concerns silencing.

What is silenced is *reason* rather than *people*. Many people talk long and loud, but that does not mean that they communicate or exchange ideas. Too many people talk too much without employing any reasoned arguments at all. Often people pretend to give reasons without really supplying any decent reasons whatsoever. Many have just given up on providing, expecting or even listening to reasons. The result is what also bothered Paul Simon and Art Garfunkel when they sang about the sound of silence in 1964: People exchanging hot air without understanding each other.

Why try when you cannot succeed?

According to a Pew Research Center survey,

> Both Republicans and Democrats are about as likely to say
> that talking about politics with people whom they disagree

with is 'stressful and frustrating' as say such conversations are 'interesting and informative'. And majorities in
both parties (65 per cent of Republicans, 63 per cent of
Democrats) say that when they talk to people on the
other side, they usually end up finding they have less
in common politically than they thought.[1]

In order to avoid pointless stress, people often just give up
and don't even try to articulate or digest information or
reasons.

The resulting silence has been well documented.[2] Research
has also shown that disadvantaged groups are more often and
more fully silenced than dominant groups.[3] However, silence
infects both sides in political debates. Neither side can claim
to be alone in being silenced – or to be alone in being frus-
trated by attempts to reach the other side. As a result, they
both quit trying to reason with each other.

Where did you hear that?

Even without talking together, people can still access arguments on the opposing side if they listen to news and commentary from the same sources as their opponents. However,
few people want to get their news from sources that abuse
and distort their political views. They reject such sources as
subjective or even 'fake news'. Most people prefer to have
their views supported, so they choose news sources that will
back up their predilections.

This trend affects both sides of the political spectrum. In
2004, Republicans and Democrats watched MSNBC and Fox

News at roughly equal rates. By 2008, 20 per cent more Democrats watched MSNBC than Republicans. On the other hand, Republicans watched Fox News 11 per cent more than Democrats in 2004, but 30 per cent more than Democrats in 2008.[4] Both sides had turned to different news shows in only four short years!

Many people today get their news from the internet. The most common tools for choosing which parts of the internet to access are search engines and social media. When someone googles a topic, the search engine lists sites about that subject in a certain order, according to an algorithm. The most common search engines give priority to sites that this user has visited often and is likely to rate highly. If users go more often to sites listed on top, as most people do, then they are bound to end up visiting more sites that support their political views. Many are not even aware that algorithms can manipulate them into echo chambers.

Another tool for selecting websites – word of mouth (so to speak) in social media – might be even more common.[5] Many people use social media to recommend websites, and their friends then follow their recommendations. In this case, it is obvious why liberals with liberal friends end up visiting websites of liberal news sources, whereas conservatives with conservative friends end up visiting websites of conservative news sources. Both sides end up in echo chambers, and they hear nothing that comes from outside those chambers. The edge of each person's echo chamber is where silence begins.[6]

Some brave souls do seek conflicting news sources. However, their motive is often simply to find mistakes there in order to criticize those sources, instead of learning from them. They are not really listening, but simply waiting to pounce. One master of this technique was Jon Stewart, the host of *The Daily Show*. He could always find short clips that made Fox News look silly. Of course, these clips were often unfair, because they had been ripped out of context. Stewart's excuse was that his show was comedy, not serious news, but he still set a tone for his viewers. When they did listen to opposing news sources, each side was trained to laugh at the bad parts instead of learning from the good parts of their political opponents.

If fellow citizens get their facts as well as analysis and commentary from conflicting sources, then it is no wonder that they end up consistently supporting opposite positions. It is also not surprising that they despise people who disagree with them, because those people seem ignorant of the most basic and central facts that have been all over the news – at least the news that they watch.

What good can questions do?

If opponents are so ignorant, there is little to be gained by asking them why they believe what they do. This is one explanation for the fact that many people today have stopped asking each other for reasons.

Another explanation for the demise of questioning is cultural. In some circles, it is disdained as naive or impolite to ask someone why they think and act as they do – for example when religion is being discussed. Religious beliefs affect people's stands on many crucial and divisive issues. But what happens when a Muslim walks into the room? Does anyone ask that Muslim why they believe that the Koran is a Holy Book? Or why they believe that Muhammad was a prophet? I have never heard anyone ask that question in such a situation, maybe because they do not expect any useful or reasoned answer. Instead, people either avoid the subject of religion and talk about something else, or they avoid the Muslim and assume that he or she is sympathetic to terrorism. Neither approach accomplishes anything. Both sides remain completely ignorant of any reasons behind the other side's position on the elephant in the room: religion. And the same goes for Christians, Jews, Hindus and atheists.

Consider also gay marriage. Among my liberal friends in Europe and the US, if anyone were to say that governments should not recognize gay marriages, then that person would immediately be labelled a bigot and ostracized. If anyone bothered to ask 'Why shouldn't gay marriages be recognized?' the questioner would be ready to jump all over any answer that a conservative gave. They would not listen sympathetically, interpret charitably, or look for any truth in that opponent's reply.

In return, conservatives dismiss gay marriage as disgusting, immoral or unnatural, and then they dismiss its advocates as dupes of gay advocacy groups. They assume that the United States Supreme Court opinions in support of a constitutional right to gay marriage are totally political, the products of judicial overreach – even before they read the arguments in those opinions.[7] Why bother reading the judicial opinions carefully when you are already confident that they are wrong? Attitudes like these keep people on either side from digging deeper into the reasoning on both sides.

Moreover, even when people do ask questions, they are often ignored and not answered. Just watch any political debate. A moderator asks a serious question, then the candidate proceeds to talk about something entirely separate. Sometimes this non-response is portrayed as background information, but the speaker never gets back to answering the original question. Sometimes they simply change the subject with no excuse whatsoever. Either way, the tendency not to *answer* questions contributes to the tendency not to *ask* questions either. Why bother asking a question when it is unlikely to elicit any real response? The only kinds of questions that end up being asked are rhetorical questions whose answers are already obvious – or thought to be obvious – so nobody bothers to give or listen to the answer. 'The rest is silence' (as Hamlet said as he died).

What good can arguments do?

Even if we do not want to be silent or silenced ourselves, we still might want to silence others. Many of my liberal friends not only dislike conservatives – they *like* to dislike them. They think that they should dislike conservatives. They are proud of their refusal to reason or even talk with their opponents. They ask, 'Why should we try to understand *them*? Why should we be civil to *them*? We need to fight them, and abuse is a weapon worth wielding. If we can silence them, so much the better.' Of course, conservatives reply in kind. They think that liberals deserve the abuse that they heap on them, because liberals are threatening the well-being of their country as well as the values that conservatives hold dear. They would be happy if liberals shut up. Their goal is to silence the opposition.

Perhaps not everyone should get along. Maybe a few like-minded friends are enough or even better than trying to like everyone. When extreme danger is imminent, some enemies need to be stopped with laws or even guns instead of just words.

Still, we would lose a lot if we never encountered worthy opponents. If everybody agreed with us, or if we talked only to allies and never left our echo chambers, then we would never look for any new evidence to counter opposition. Our lack of exposure to any arguments on the other side would make us overconfident. It would also reduce our ability to correct mistakes, so we would become more likely to get stuck in a rut.

This basic point was made long ago by John Stuart Mill in *On Liberty*. Mill also saw other advantages of deliberating with a variety of interlocutors. When we need to deliberate with opponents, we are forced to present arguments for our positions, and thereby gain a better understanding of our own positions and the reasons for them. One recent study found, 'incongruent information increases thought quality as measured by thoughts' integrative complexity, volume of thoughts, and frequency of arguments'.[8] Improvements were made in reasoning that supported prior beliefs, but better arguments can also enhance understanding of that position by both sides – advocates as well as opponents. We become more justified in believing what we do, and our views become more nuanced, subtle and refined after we add qualifications, even if we hold onto basically the same positions that we started with. Encounters with opponents help us in many ways.

To find counter-evidence and counter-arguments whenever possible, we need to seek groups whose members vary in as many relevant ways as possible.[9] It also helps for the groups to engage in extended and respectful deliberation.[10] Today we have new tools to help us accomplish this goal. We can use the internet to facilitate encounters with opposing views, for example by joining deliberative groups of people whom we would rarely encounter otherwise, or by deploying digital tools such as Reddit's thread, 'ChangeMyView'.[11]

The goal is not to get everyone to agree. How boring that would be! Diversity of opinion invigorates and illuminates. Nor is the goal to make us all open to other positions. We should not be willing to move to a new position that is clearly mistaken. Instead, the goal is to remain civil, understand opponents, and learn from them even when they are mistaken.

Of course, there is no guarantee that mixed groups who deliberate will arrive at mutual respect, much less the truth or the best policies. Some risk of error is unavoidable. Still, reasoning with opponents gives us more chance of arriving at mutual understanding and respect as well as true beliefs and good policies.

Isn't silence soothing?

If reason should not be silenced, do we have to talk about controversial issues all day long? No. Excessive arguing can create problems of its own. Most of the time we should leave controversies alone and get on with more pleasant parts of our lives.

Internet trolls sometimes engage in what is called 'sea-lioning'. They demand that you keep arguing with them for as long they want you to, even long after you realize that further discussion is pointless. If you announce that you want to stop, then they accuse you of being closed-minded or opposed to reason. This practice is obnoxious. Reason should not be silenced, but it needs to take a vacation sometimes.

When we do talk about controversial issues, we do not always have to include opponents in our discussions. Many universities in the US have set up 'safe spaces' where students can go if they want to talk about intimate and controversial issues without encountering opposition or scepticism. These environments are supposed to be supportive and to aid healing and improve self-confidence, especially in groups that are often dismissed or denounced by others. Gay students, for example, get tired of defending their lifestyle in hostile environments, so they can gain personal strength from entering a safe space where they know people will not call them immoral. Such safe spaces are perfectly compatible with my general point that we need to encounter opponents in order to learn from them. There is enough time in life for both. Nothing is wrong with using safe spaces at certain times in order to prepare ourselves to encounter opponents at other times – as long as everyone eventually does get out and encounter opposition often enough to understand that opposition.

Even when the time is right, what is valuable is not simply talking about controversies – we need to learn to talk to opponents in the right way. The Rapoport rules (quoted above) explain part of what counts as the right way. Parts Two and Three of this book say more about what is the right

What Arguments Can Do

Arguments cannot solve our problems all by themselves. Even good seed cannot grow on infertile soil, so audiences must be receptive before arguments can accomplish anything. To nurture their receptivity, we need many other virtues, including modesty, graciousness, civility, patience and forgiveness. But if all of that has to be present in advance, what further good can arguments really do that these other virtues have not already done?

Who is the slave?

Many cynics and sceptics will dismiss reasoning right from the start. They deny that reason and argument have as much power as I claim. Sometimes these sceptics deny that reason and argument have any power at all. In their view, reason does nothing – because they believe that emotion does it all. According to them, we are driven completely by our emotions, feelings and desires rather than by reason or beliefs – much less arguments.

In support of this view, such critics often quote the early modern philosopher David Hume, who notoriously said, 'Reason is and ought only to be the slave of the passions.'[1]

This simple slogan is catchy, but Hume's considered views are much more complex and subtle:

> [I]n order to pave the way for such a sentiment [or emotion], and give a proper discernment of its object, it is often necessary, we find, that much reasoning should precede, that nice distinctions be made, just conclusions drawn, distant comparisons formed, complicated relations examined, and general facts fixed and ascertained . . . [I]n many orders of beauty, particularly those of the finer arts, it is requisite to employ much reasoning, in order to feel the proper sentiment; and a false relish may frequently be corrected by argument and reflection. There are just grounds to conclude, that moral beauty partakes much of this latter species, and demands the assistance of our intellectual faculties, in order to give it a suitable influence on the human mind.[2]

Hume here explains how reasoning often precedes, influences and corrects emotions, especially on moral matters. If reason is a slave, this slave sometimes guides its master.

One lesson from Hume's passage is that the contrast between reason and emotion is a false dichotomy. We need not – and should not – hold either that emotion does everything and reason does nothing, or that reason does everything and emotion does nothing. Instead, emotion can be guided by reason. Indeed, emotions can be reasons, such as when fear indicates danger or happiness is evidence of having made a good choice. And strong emotion can be backed by strong reasons, such as when I get very angry that someone raped my friend. Reason does not always require us to remain calm and cold. The rational and emotional aspects of our nature do and should work together as allies in shaping our judgements and decisions. They need not conflict or compete.

Hume was analysing moral and aesthetic judgements, but his point applies as well to personal, political and religious disputes. Cynics often claim that people pick their friends, political parties and religious stances on the basis of their feelings – fear, anger, hatred and disgust, but also positive attraction. They feel their way into their positions instead of reasoning or thinking about facts. They move from 'ought' to 'is' – from their beliefs about how the world ought to be to beliefs that the world really is that way.

Of course, nobody denies or should deny that emotion is crucial to hot issues. Emotion is what makes hot issues hot. Nonetheless, reason and argument also have some role to play. People would not become active and risk alienating others if they did not feel strongly about their personal, political or religious positions. At the same time, they might not feel that way if they did not think and reason about the relevant facts in the ways they do. Reason thereby affects actions, because actions are based on motivations and emotions, and those motivations and emotions are shaped by beliefs and reasoning.

To see this in a personal example, just imagine that an informant tells you that your rival for promotion in your job lied about you to your bosses, and then she got the promotion instead of you. 'That demon! I hate her! I am going to get back at her!' Your emotions are aroused, and they lead you to undermine her career. Your anger leads you to lie about her, but you are caught. Your boss then fires you for undermining her and the group.

The fact that your acts were so counterproductive and destructive would lead many to tag your acts as irrational and emotional. Emotions are seen as preventing reasoning that would have stopped you from getting into trouble. You would never act that way towards your rival if you did not have those emotions.

Still, you would also never have acted in that way if you did not believe that your rival had lied about you and that her lie was the reason you did not get the promotion. You trust your informant, so you reasoned from his report to reach the conclusion that your rival lied about you. Then you assumed that her lie was the best explanation for your failure to get promoted. This reasoning was what led you to feel strong negative emotions towards your rival. If you had not trusted your informant – or if you had not believed that your rival's lie made any difference to your promotion – you would not have been nearly so angry and vengeful. Then you would have kept your job.

In this way, reason and emotion together shape behaviour. Emotions sometimes arise from aspects of the situation that have little or nothing to do with the relevant facts. However, we usually get mad at people because we believe that they have done something wrong. Our anger might then lead us to act in irrational ways, but it arises originally from a belief about the other person, and that belief can be the product of the process of reasoning. If the reasoning is faulty, then the emotion is unjustified and can lead us astray. Even if the reasoning is good, the emotion can become so strong that it prevents reasoning later on. Either way, we need to take account of both reasoning and emotion in order to understand the action. It is a mistake to think that the act results from either reason or emotion alone.

The same point holds at the social level in politics. Consider the recent Brexit vote in the UK. Opponents of Brexit, who lost the referendum, claimed that the vote was fuelled by emotions – fear of immigration, frustration with politicians and so on – which made voters forget or ignore the arguments for the economic costs of Brexit. This pattern is common. Voters who lose typically say that their opponents acted on emotion instead of reason. But think about it. There really were a lot of immigrants flooding into Europe and Britain.[3] They really did have an impact on British citizens. It is true that the vote might have gone differently if British citizens had welcomed them instead of fearing them. But it is also true that the outcome of the vote would have been different if the facts had been different, for example if there had been fewer immigrants – assuming that citizens would have changed their beliefs accordingly. The vote might also have gone the other way if the British people had been convinced that the immigrants were helping them instead of taking their jobs and using up public services. These matters need to be decided by cognition, reasoning and argument. Thus, both arguments to settle the facts and emotions to see how we react to those facts play a role in determining the response. Here there is no either/or. Cynical commentators have gone too far to emphasize emotions and downplay reasoning. Reason also plays a role – not instead of but in addition to emotion.

In many cases like these, reason is not the slave of the passions, nor is passion the slave of reason. Instead of being slaves and masters, they work together as peers and allies – or at least they can.

Is there any hope?

Critics of this point of view will not give up yet. Sure, they will admit, our beliefs guide our emotions. But why think that reasoning or arguments really determine our beliefs? Our beliefs might just be post-hoc rationalizations that we make up to fit our feelings. We might really believe what we do because we want to believe that. Or we might believe it for no reason at all. Then reason and argument have nothing to do with what we believe.

This sentiment has been expressed by cynics through the ages who deny that arguments do any good:

> I have come to the conclusion that there is only one way under high heaven to get the best of an argument – and that is to avoid it. Avoid it as you would avoid rattlesnakes and earthquakes. *Dale Carnegie*[4]

> Arguments are to be avoided, they are always vulgar and often convincing. *Oscar Wilde*[5]

Witty, huh?

It is fun to make such extreme claims, but now we need to ask whether they are correct or accurate. Of course not: they are snarky exaggerations. The truth is that, although we cannot always reason with everyone, that limitation does not prove that arguments and reasoning are never useful.

Admittedly, arguing (especially online) can be frustrating.

Opponents often do not listen at all. But they do listen sometimes. I used to think that mammals did not lay eggs. Then I read on Wikipedia that monotremes are mammals that lay eggs. I could have resisted, but I didn't. I reasoned my way to the conclusion that some mammals lay eggs, because I wanted to get it right.

I didn't care much about monotremes – but some arguments can change our lives in major ways and lead us to act contrary to basic desires. Once I taught a course on applied ethics that discussed animal rights and vegetarianism. After the course, one student thanked me by saying, 'Your course has made my whole family happier.' His parents were both vegetarians, but he had not been a vegetarian himself. During the course, he had come to appreciate the arguments for vegetarianism, so he understood his parents better. Moreover, he decided to become a vegetarian. 'Why?' I asked. He claimed that the arguments on that side seemed stronger to him. Of course, he could have been deluded. It is possible that the arguments really had no effect. Perhaps he really wanted to get along better with his family. It's possible, but he reported that he already got along with them very well. Maybe some horrific picture of animals suffering in a factory farm is what really turned him around. And yet I did not show any horrific pictures of animals suffering in factory farms, and he did not report seeing such pictures himself (and why would he lie or forget?). In this case, then, the arguments did at least some of the work. He became a vegetarian because the arguments gave him reasons to become a vegetarian.

Many other examples of radical conversion in the light of evidence are well documented. Megan Phelps-Roper reports that she gave up her allegiance to Westboro Baptist Church partly because:

> My friends on Twitter took the time to understand Westboro's doctrines, and in doing so, they were able to find inconsistencies I'd missed my entire life. Why did we advocate the death penalty for gays when Jesus said, 'Let he who is without sin cast the first stone?' How could we claim to love our neighbour while at the same time praying for God to destroy them? The truth is that the care shown to me by these strangers on the internet was itself a contradiction. It was growing evidence that people on the other side were not the demons I'd been led to believe.[6]

Of course, her emotions towards her Twitter friends as well as her compassion for her neighbours played a large role in her conversion. But that does not mean that reason played no role. Her emotion made her listen to her Twitter friends, but she reports that the content of what they said also made a difference: 'they were able to find inconsistencies'. She was convinced by 'growing evidence'.

Admittedly, other members of Westboro Baptist Church did not change their beliefs. Maybe they did not listen. This shows that arguments are not always enough by themselves to ensure a certain belief or action. But nobody should expect that much. A match does not light every time you strike it. Sometimes the match or the matchbook is wet. Sometimes there is not enough friction where you strike it. Sometimes there is not enough oxygen. Moreover, sometimes the match lights without striking, such as when you light one match with another match. Thus, a cause does not have to be

strictly necessary or sufficient for the effect in all circumstances. Nonetheless, when the match does light, striking the
match is what causes it to light. Analogously, giving someone
an argument for a conclusion can cause the audience to
believe that conclusion.

Then why do cynics deny that arguments affect beliefs?
This simplistic view is appealing because everyone has had
the frustrating experience of giving a good argument that
convinces nobody. But what does that show? Perhaps only
that no one listened or understood. Maybe only that the argument was not as good as it seemed. Possibly only that the audience needed time to mull it over.

Cynicism results from unrealistic expectations. If we expect an argument to be a knock-down proof that convinces
everyone immediately on first hearing, then we are bound to
be disappointed. Almost no arguments work like that. If we
trim our expectations to make them more realistic, and if we
are patient enough to wait for effects that take a while instead
of demanding immediate capitulation, then we will find that
reasons and arguments can have some influence. Sometimes
some arguments do change some people's beliefs and actions
slowly and partially. That weak claim might disappoint cynics
who demand more, but it might also be enough to give us
hope for progress.

What do we get out of arguing?

My overall goal here is to show how fascinating and important arguments are and to undermine common misunderstandings about reasons and arguments. Most people see

arguments as ways to persuade other people or to beat them in some kind of verbal fight, debate or competition. That view is not all wrong, but it is limited and incomplete. Some people do present arguments as displays of prowess or power, but arguments can also play more constructive roles in social interactions.

LEARNING

Imagine that I argue with you about negotiations regarding sanctions against North Korea. I argue that China should be kept out of the negotiations. You argue that China should be allowed into the negotiations, because China will make the sanctions more effective. You refute my arguments and convince me that China should be brought in. If arguments are like fights or competitions, then you won. You convinced me. I did not convince you.

This view is backwards. You did not win much, if anything. After all, you ended up with the same view that you started with. You might not have learned anything because you refuted all of my arguments against your position. You might not even understand me or my initial position any better. Thus you gained little or nothing from our interaction, except perhaps some good feeling about winning a competition or showing me the error of my ways. That is why I doubt that you won.

In contrast, I gained a lot. I improved my view. I gained new evidence and new arguments. I understood the situation and my new position better than I did before our arguments. If what I wanted was truth, reason and understanding, then I got what I wanted. That makes me the real winner. Instead of resenting the person who refuted my arguments, I should thank them for teaching me. But to see why, we need to realize that arguments are not like fights, debates or competitions.

RESPECT

Another positive benefit of providing an argument or of asking for an argument is that doing so expresses respect for one's audience. When you are walking your dog on a leash, and the dog turns left when you want to turn right, what do you do? You pull on the leash. What do you *not* do? You do not say, 'Fido, listen to reason.'

Contrast walking your dog with walking with your partner. Your plan is to go for a pleasant evening stroll around the block in a city that you are visiting for the first time. When you get to an intersection, your partner turns left when you want to turn right. What do you do? You had better not just pull your partner to the right. Instead, you would, I hope, reason with your partner. You might say something like, 'I think our hotel is in this direction.' If they disagree, you might argue, 'Didn't we turn right, then right again, and then right again? If I remember that much correctly, then now we need to turn right in order to get back. Don't you agree?' You present reasons for turning right instead of just forcing your partner to turn right. The aim of giving reasons is not simply to get them to turn in the way that you want. The purpose is also to show them that you appreciate that they can understand and respond to those reasons, unlike a dog. It also shows them that you recognize that you might be wrong and they might be right. You give them a chance to respond by showing that you are wrong or that something is wrong with your argument. This kind of exchange of reasons happens between equals who respect each other and admit their own fallibility. One benefit of providing an argument is to signal that you see your relationship to the other person in this light.

The signal is sent not only when we *give* a reason but also when we *ask* for a reason. It can get very annoying when a child asks 'Why?' after everything you say. Still, it can also be annoying when someone does *not* ask why you disagree with them. You say, 'Let's turn right.' Your partner responds, 'No. Let's turn left.' That's it. Nothing more. That would annoy most people, partly because we want other people to recognize that they owe us a reason, but also because we want them to be interested in our reasons. To ask 'Why do you want to turn right?' is to show a recognition that I am the kind of creature who can give a reason. It is a sign of respect.

HUMILITY

In addition to showing respect, another benefit of using reason and argument is that they can foster humility. If two people disagree without arguing, all they do is yell at each other. No progress is made. Both still think that they are right. In contrast, if both sides cite arguments that articulate reasons for their positions, then new possibilities open up. One possibility is that one of the arguments gets refuted – that is, shown to fail. In that case, the person who depended on the refuted argument learns that he needs to change his view. That is one way to achieve humility – on one side at least. Another possibility is that neither argument is refuted. Both have a degree of reason on their side. Even if neither interlocutor is convinced by the other's argument, both can still come to appreciate the opposing view. They also realize that, even if they have some truth, they do not have the whole truth. They can gain humility when they recognize and appreciate the reasons for opposing their own view.

How can arguments induce such humility? The best way to reduce opponents' overconfidence and make them more susceptible to your position might seem to be to make an overwhelming argument that shows them why they are wrong and why you are right. Sometimes that works, but only rarely.

What usually works better is to ask questions – in particular, to ask opponents for reasons. Questions are often more powerful than assertions. But which questions? We need to learn to ask the right kinds of questions, the ones that lead to productive conversations. In one experiment, Steven Sloman, professor of psychology at Brown University, and his colleagues found that, broadly speaking, asking people *why* they hold their beliefs leads to less humility and openness to conflicting views than asking them *how* their proposal works.[7] The question of how cap and trade policies reduce global warming, for example, asks subjects to spell out a causal mechanism step-by-step. Subjects found it difficult to specify this mechanism, so they came to realize that they did not understand their own position well enough, and they became more moderate and open to alternative views. We can also ask ourselves similar questions. Questioning how our own plans are supposed to work will likely make us more humble and open-minded, because then we come to realize that we do not understand as much as we thought or as much as we need to.

Moreover, if we regularly ask others and ourselves such

questions, then we will probably come to anticipate such questions in advance. Jennifer Lerner and Philip Tetlock, psychologists at Harvard University and the University of Pennsylvania, respectively, have shown that accountability – expecting to need to give reasons for claims – leads people to base their positions more on relevant facts than on personal likes and dislikes.[8] A context that creates such expectations – including a culture that encourages asking such questions about reasons – could then help to foster humility, understanding, reasoning and arguments that give answers to questions about reasons.

The goal of questioning and humility is not to make one lose confidence in cases where confidence is justified. Proper humility does not require one to lose all self-confidence, to give up all beliefs, or to grovel or debase oneself. One can still hold one's beliefs strongly while recognizing that there are reasons to believe otherwise, that one might be wrong, and that one does not have the whole truth. Giving and expecting reasons along with asking and answering questions can help move us in this direction.

ABSTRACTION

Arguments can also undermine polarization. If people are more humble and modest, they are less likely to adopt extreme positions. They are also less likely to be so sure of their own positions that they think of their opponents as stupid or immoral, so they will not be so abusive and antagonistic.

There is also a less obvious way in which argument undermines polarization: it leads people to think more abstractly. When people formulate arguments for their position, for example their political stance, they usually appeal to abstract principles, such as general rights. Another method is to use analogies, but those analogies tend to rely on abstract similarities between otherwise distinct cases. Thus many common forms of argument require people to step back from details of a particular case and think about the issues from a more abstract perspective.

Abstract thinking then reduces polarization, at least in the right context. When people think about a political issue, they can think of themselves either as a citizen of their country or as a member of their particular political party. Research has shown that, when people identify with a particular political party, abstract thinking can increase polarization. In contrast, when people identify with their country as a whole, abstract thinking decreases polarization between groups inside that country.[9] The mechanism behind this effect is unclear, but people who think abstractly in terms of their country appeal both to principles that bind together the whole country and also to interests that they share with other citizens. These appeals have, of course, just as much force for many of their opponents within their country, so the result is less polarization and more mutual understanding.

Of course, abstraction need not stop here. It is also possible for people to identify with their species, so that they view themselves as a human like other humans, extending the scope of their appeal across other countries. I would speculate that abstract thinking in this perspective might even help to overcome antagonism and polarization between countries.

The evidence does not suggest that political opponents

will suddenly become best friends as soon as they think about their own arguments and those of their opponents. We need to be more patient than that. Nonetheless, a cultural shift towards more use of argument and a better appreciation of the arguments might have some effect on polarization by inducing more abstract thinking.

COMPROMISE

Last but not least, arguments can enable compromises. If I know your reasons for disagreeing with me, and you know my reasons for disagreeing with you, then we can work together to find an intermediate position that satisfies both of our concerns. Imagine that you favour an increase in the minimum wage because anyone who works full-time should not live in poverty, whereas I oppose increasing the minimum wage because it will reduce the number of jobs for the poor. You are concerned about poverty among workers, and I am concerned about jobs. Knowing our reasons, we can seek a compromise position that will raise as many workers as possible above poverty without costing too many jobs. If we had not given our reasons (if we had omitted the 'because clauses'), then we would not know where to look for a compromise that we can both live with.

You might ask, 'So what? Why do we need compromise anyway?' Although 82 per cent of consistent liberals prefer leaders who compromise, 63 per cent of consistent conservatives prefer leaders who stick to their principles.[10] Both positions can cite support. Failure to compromise can lead to war; but nevertheless some compromises are rotten.[11] Famous examples in the US include the Three-Fifths Compromise (which counted slaves as three-fifths of a person in calculating the population of states) and the Missouri Compromise (which allowed slavery in some areas but not others). The most infamous example in Europe is Neville Chamberlain's appeasement of Hitler. There are instances – as in the cases of slavery and Hitler – in which we should not compromise. However, does this admission apply to compromises today? If people really hate their rivals as much as slavery and Hitler, then they might have reason to oppose such terrible compromises. But then the basic problem is that the two sides hate each other as much as slavery and Hitler. Without that extreme assumption, compromise would often be desirable.

Of course, no compromise is perfect. Compromise is not easy. It is not ideal. It is not without dangers. But it is still necessary. We need to be able to compromise in some cases in order to get anything done. The best compromises are constructive in the sense that they create more value and leave both sides better off. Competing parties will not know how to fashion such compromises unless they know what the other side values – and the best way to learn their values and thereby to facilitate compromise is to listen carefully to their reasons and arguments.

Where do we stand now?

The problem of polarization pervades politics and cultures around the world today, as we saw in previous chapters. This chapter suggests that a better understanding of arguments and the reasons that they express can go some way towards ameliorating those problems. Why? Because reasoning and

From Why to How

CHAPTER 5

Why Learn How to Argue?

Many people believe that they already know how to argue: they simply proclaim a reason for their position. They also believe that they are good at it because the reasons that they give seem strong to them. And they believe that they can tell a bad argument from a good one just by thinking about it.

If arguing and assessing arguments were really this easy, there would be no need for the rest of this book. You would not need to learn how to argue. You would already know how.

Arguing well is not that simple. Indeed, most people are pretty bad at arguing in many circumstances. They make the same mistakes over and over again. These tendencies do not result from ignorance or lack of intelligence. Even smart people endorse and get fooled by bad arguments if they have not been trained properly. That is why we all need to work hard at learning how to argue.

Do you want to make a deal?

Paradoxes show how much we have to learn. This became evident when Marilyn vos Savant, a famous mathematician, challenged her readers to solve the Monty Hall problem (named after the host of the American game show *Let's Make a Deal*; also known as the Three-Door problem):

> Suppose you're on a game show, and you're given the choice of three doors: behind one door is a car; behind the others, goats. You pick, say No. 1, and the host, who knows what's behind the doors, opens another door, say No. 3, which has a goat. He then says to you, 'Do you want to pick door No. 2?' Is it to your advantage to switch your choice?[1]

Most readers, including several mathematics professors, answered that there is no advantage in switching. This reply appears to be correct because only two doors (No. 1 and No. 2) remain closed, you know that one hides a goat and the other hides a car, and you seem to have no reason to think that one door is more likely than the other to hide the car.

But this is misleading. To understand why, recall that there are only three possible arrangements behind the three doors: car-goat-goat, goat-car-goat or goat-goat-car. If you pick door No. 1 initially, and then Monty Hall reveals a goat behind one of the other doors, you will win a car two times out of three by switching. You lose by switching to door No. 2 or No. 3 only in the first order (car-goat-goat), but you would win in both of the other two orders (goat-car-goat and goat-goat-car).

Experts now agree on this solution (i.e. switching is best), but not everybody is convinced. That is exactly the point here. We are not as good at reasoning as we would like to think. We need to learn how to do better.

Will your wishes come true?

Psychological studies also show us why we need to work on our skills. In some of these experiments, the question is whether an argument is valid in the sense that it is not possible for its premises to be true when its conclusion is false. The results reveal how many people assess an argument as valid because they want its conclusion to be true.[2] Consider this argument: 'If the referees are unfair, then Manchester United will lose. The referees will be fair. So Manchester United will win.' Many Manchester United fans will probably believe that this argument is valid. This belief is incorrect, however, because its premises are true but its conclusion is false if the referees will be fair but Manchester United will lose anyway. It is possible that Manchester will lose regardless of whether or not the referees are fair. The fans' mistake results from their reluctance to imagine the possibility of their team losing, which they want to avoid. That is why fans of rivals of Manchester United make this mistake less often. They are happy to admit the possibility of Manchester United losing regardless of the referees. Of course, that does not mean that they are smarter or more logical than Manchester United fans, because they will make the same mistake about their own favourite team. Both sides engage in wishful thinking.

A related weakness is desirability bias, which is the tendency to seek out information that supports positions you want to be true.[3] Recall the last time you stepped on a scale to see how much you weighed. Studies show that if the scale shows a weight that you like, then you will be more likely to believe it; but if the scale shows a weight that you do not like, then you are more likely to step off and step back on the scale in the hope that it will show a better weight the second time. We all do something like this.

Can you trust representatives?

Our reasoning and arguments are also led astray by heuristics. Daniel Kahneman, a Princeton University professor who won the Nobel Prize in Economic Sciences, called one classic heuristic, *representativeness*. Kahneman and his collaborators gave participants this description of a graduate student:

> Tom W. is of high intelligence, although lacking in true creativity. He has a need for order and clarity, and for neat and tidy systems in which every detail finds its appropriate place. His writing is rather dull and mechanical, occasionally enlivened by somewhat corny puns and by flashes of imagination of the sci-fi type. He has a strong drive for competence. He seems to have little feel and little sympathy for other people and does not enjoy interacting with others. Self-centered, he nonetheless has a deep moral sense.[4]

Participants were given a list of nine fields of graduate study. One group of participants were asked to rank those fields by the degree to which Tom 'resembles a typical graduate student' in each field. Another group was asked to rank the fields by the likelihood that Tom is in each field. Both groups were also asked to estimate the percentage of graduate students in each of the nine fields. These estimates varied from

3 per cent to 20 per cent, and Tom's description reflected the stereotype of the smaller fields, such as library science. Nonetheless, participants' percentage estimates had almost no effect on their probability rankings. Instead, the answers to the questions about representativeness and probability were almost perfectly correlated. This suggests that these subjects neglected the baseline percentage and based their probability estimates almost totally on their judgements of representativeness. They ignored crucial information that should have altered their reasoning.

Should you turn over a new leaf?

Another common error arises in the Wason selection task. Participants see four cards with a letter on one side and a number on the other side, and one side facing up:

Then participants are told a rule:

> If a card has B on one side, then it has 2 on the other side.

The task is to turn over the minimum cards needed to determine whether the rule is true. The correct answer is to turn over the cards that show B and 9, because the rule is false if the B card does not have a 2 on its reverse or if the 9 card has a B on its reverse. Unfortunately, studies consistently find that most university students (as high as 90 per cent) do not turn over the B and 9 cards. Most turn over either the B card alone or the B and 2 cards. However, there is no need to turn over the 2 card, because the rule will not be falsified whether or not there is a B on the other side. After all, the rule says only what is on the other side of cards that *do* have a B on one side. It does not say what is on the reverse of cards that do *not* have a B on one side.

Fortunately, this mistake becomes much less common when the task is transferred to a practical context. Suppose the cards look like this:

| Beer | Water | 15 | 25 |

Then participants are told that each card has the customer's age on one side and what that customer drank on the other side, and the law is:

> If a customer is less than twenty-one years old, they are not allowed to drink beer.

The task here is to turn over the minimum cards needed to determine which customers are breaking the law. Participants do much better on this more practical task. Some researchers explain this success by our evolutionary history. We evolved to determine when social rules (such as laws) are violated, but not to test pointless generalizations (such as whether cards with B on one side have 2 on the other side).[5]

Can we get better?

These experiments (and many more) show that we are far from perfect reasoners. Duh! We already knew that. They also specify particular ways in which people often go astray. That is interesting, and it helps us know when we need to be careful.

The fact that we often get misled does not show that we cannot ever reason properly. Tricky psychologists set up special circumstances in order to get participants to make mistakes. Nonetheless, the Wason selection task shows that we can do better in certain circumstances (practical ones) than in others (abstract ones). Moreover, we can recognize when we have made mistakes. After people give the wrong answer on the Wason selection task, it is easy to show them why their answer is wrong. They rarely stick to their original answer. That shows that we can learn and that we can distinguish good reasoning from bad reasoning in suitable circumstances.

Other psychologists have found that different situations are more conducive to proper reasoning. Despite their failures while alone, participants in groups gave around 80 per cent correct answers in the Wason selection task; and more generally 'people are quite capable of reasoning in an unbiased manner, at least when they are evaluating arguments rather than producing them, and when they are after the truth instead of trying to win a debate'.[6] In addition, institutions (such as science) can be structured so as to maximize the chances that errors will be discovered and rejected, so that they will not be led astray in the long run.[7] Thus, we can improve reasoning and argument not only by training but also by instilling a desire for truth and understanding as well as by creating institutions that correct mistakes. Those circumstances are more likely in a culture that understands reasons and arguments.

Our skills at reasoning and argument are both prone to error and correctable. The glass is not only half full or only half empty – it is both. It takes hard and careful work as well as patience and tenacity to get better at arguing and reasoning. Although difficult and not always successful,[8] training and practice in argument and reasoning can help people recognize their mistakes, and they can also help people avoid mistakes in reasoning.[9] That is why we all need to work hard at learning how to argue.

PART TWO

How to Argue

How to Spot Arguments

We seem to argue all the time. People disagree on many issues and let each other know it, often at high volume. On the other hand, people too rarely give reasons for their positions. In that sense, arguments are not very common and not common enough. So, are arguments numerous or rare? That depends on what counts as an argument. This chapter will explore that question.

How much would you pay for an argument?

In order to understand what an argument is, we need to begin by asking what an argument is *not*. Some of the main contrasts are illustrated by an insightful troupe of philosophers named Monty Python in their famous skit 'The Argument Clinic'. If you have not seen it or do not remember it, you should watch it.[1] It is a gem.

The skit begins with a customer walking up to the receptionist in the clinic and saying, 'I'd like to have an argument, please.' The receptionist replies, 'It's one pound for a five-minute argument, but only eight pounds for a course of ten.'

Despite the savings in bulk, the customer decides to purchase only one five-minute argument.

The receptionist then needs to find an employee in the clinic to argue with the customer. She looks at the schedule and says, 'Mr Du-Bakey's free, but he's a little bit conciliatory.' What's wrong with being conciliatory – that is, likely to give in easily? Anyway, the receptionist instead directs the customer to Mr Barnard in room 12.

The customer walks down the hall and enters the first room to find Mr Barnard seated behind a desk. He aggressively yells, 'WHAT DO YOU WANT?' then calls the customer a 'snotty-faced heap of parrot droppings' and a 'vacuous, toffee-nosed, malodorous pervert'. Annoyed, the customer explains that he came for an argument. Mr Barnard nicely replies, 'Oh! I'm sorry. This is abuse . . . You want room 12A, next door.'

This silliness introduces our first contrast with arguments. Abuse is not an argument. I cannot argue for my position or against your position simply by calling you a 'pervert'. Why not? Presumably because calling you a pervert is not the same as giving you reasons why I am opposed to your position, much less any reasons for my own position. It is surprising how often people forget this simple point.[2]

Skipping ahead in the skit, the customer enters a different room, and Spreaders hits him on the head. When the customer reacts, he is told, 'No, no, no. Hold your head like this, then go Waaah.' Then Spreaders hits him again. It turns out that this room is for 'being-hit-on-the-head lessons'. This concept is absurd, but it reveals a second contrast with arguments. Arguments are not physical fights – or verbal fights. The goal of an argument is not to make an opponent's head hurt (either by hitting him hard or by making him think hard).

When the customer finally reaches the correct room, a professional arguer named Mr Vibrating is sitting behind a desk. The customer asks, 'Is this the right room for an argument?' The clinician calmly replies, 'I've told you once.' The heat rises from there: 'No, you haven't', 'Yes, I have', 'When?', 'Just now!', 'No, you didn't', 'Yes, I did', 'Didn't' . . . 'I'm telling you, I did', 'You did not'. The repetition is finally broken when the clinician asks, 'Is this a five-minute argument or the full half-hour?' Then the customer realizes what is going on: he is already arguing. Or is he? The customer and clinician continue to say Yes-No-Yes-No-Yes-No until the customer bursts out, 'Look. This isn't an arguments . . . it's just contradiction . . . an argument's not the same as contradiction.'

Now we have a third contrast with arguments. Contradiction here means denial, so the lesson is that arguments are not mere denials. If you make a claim, I cannot argue against your claim simply by saying, 'No'. It is again unfortunate how many people forget this simple lesson. They think that they can refute someone merely by denying what they say. They can't.

Why not? What is missing from a bare denial that is present in an argument? The customer tells us, 'Argument is an intellectual process. Contradiction is just the automatic gainsaying of anything the other person says.' It is not clear what makes something intellectual, but one interpretation is that an argument needs to present some kind of evidence or reason, whereas a bare denial does not present any evidence or reason against the claim that is denied. To say merely that some claim is false is not to give any evidence against it or any reason why it is false.

This point then leads to the customer's definition: 'An argument is a connected series of statements to establish a definite proposition.' This reference to establishing a proposition is a great start, but it is still not quite right. The first problem is that to establish something is to put it on a firm basis. However, some arguments are not firm or even intended to be firm. For example, if we are deciding whether to go to a park or to a museum, I might say, 'We went to the park last week, so maybe we ought to go to the museum today. What do you think?' I intend to give some reason for the proposition that we ought to go to the museum, but I need not claim that it is strong enough to establish that conclusion. Some arguments are too weak to establish anything, but they still give some reasons.

Another problem is that you cannot establish what was already established in advance. To establish a country is to create one that did not exist before. Analogously, to establish a conclusion is presumably also to bring the audience to believe what they did not believe firmly before. However, we often argue for conclusions that everybody strongly believed already. Just imagine that one mathematician had already proven the Pythagorean theorem (the square of the hypotenuse in a right triangle is equal to the sum of the squares of the other two sides). Then another mathematician comes up with a new proof that is shorter and makes fewer assumptions. Both proofs are arguments, but the purpose of proving the theorem the second time is not to convince people who did not believe the theorem. Everyone already believed it. Yet mathematicians still might want to prove it in fewer steps with fewer assumptions in order to determine why it is true and which axioms or premises its truth depends on. Their proof aims to explain the theorem but not to establish it. In this respect, Monty Python's definition is not quite right.

What is an argument?

One small change is enough to solve these problems with Monty Python's definition. We just need to replace 'establish' with 'present a reason for'. Then an argument can be defined as 'a connected series of statements intended to present a reason for a proposition'.[3] Reasons do not need to be strong or firm and can support what we already believed, so this change allows weak reasons as well as proofs of the Pythagorean theorem to count as arguments.

The statements that present a reason are called *premises*. The proposition that they are supposed to be a reason for is called a *conclusion*. Hence, we can say that an argument is a connected series of premises intended to present a reason for a conclusion.[4]

This definition tells us a lot about arguments. It specifies the *material* that arguments are made of (language, though not necessarily writing or speech), what *form* they take (premises and conclusions – declarative sentences that can be true or false) and what *purposes* they serve (to present reasons of some kind). This definition thus covers the aspects – material, form, purpose and cause – that Aristotle required for complete explanation.[5]

It also tells us what arguments are *not*. Following Monty Python's definition, ours shows how arguments differ from abuse, fights and denial. In addition, it explains why dictionaries and price tags do not include arguments, since they are not intended to present reasons for any conclusion.

Even where we do expect an argument, we are often disappointed. Speakers can spend a lot of time describing a problem or stating a position without arguing for anything. Many examples occur in political debates and interviews. It is amazing how long politicians can talk without giving any arguments. Reporters or others ask politicians questions about issues of the day. Politicians reply by talking around the issues and then abruptly announcing their stands. They make it clear how their views differ from their opponents' positions, but they still do not argue for their own positions. Our definition tells us why all of their words together do not amount to an argument. It is because they do not even try to present any reasons at all.

What purposes do arguments serve?

Reasons come in many kinds, and our definition does not specify which kind or kinds of reasons are intended in arguments. This lack of clarity, however, is a feature, not a bug. The non-specific notion of a reason enables our definition to be flexible enough to cover a variety of arguments.

Some arguments give reasons that justify belief in their conclusions. For example, if you doubt that ancestors of the Shona tribe in Zimbabwe used to rule a much larger area, then I can show you a book about the Great Zimbabwe. It will cite established facts that are premises in an argument that will give you strong reasons to believe the conclusion that ancestors of the Shona tribe in Zimbabwe indeed used to rule a much larger area. The cited facts make you justified in believing a conclusion that you did not believe before.

Other arguments give reasons that justify *actions* instead of *beliefs*. For example, if you are deciding whether to visit Beijing, then I can show you a book about the Forbidden City. This book will have pictures of the beautiful buildings and artifacts that you can see if you tour Beijing. This book will provide reasons for you to visit Beijing. Of course, I could also cite other facts, such as those about air pollution in Beijing, to give you a reason *not* to visit Beijing or maybe to give you a reason to visit Beijing in August instead of December. These reasons for action can also be presented in arguments.

It is important that both kinds of justification are distinct from mere persuasion. Imagine that I trick you into believing that ancestors of the Shona tribe in Zimbabwe used to rule a much larger area by showing you a book of pictures of the Forbidden City and somehow convincing you that they are pictures of a monument in Zimbabwe called the Great Zimbabwe. I am not trying to give any real reason, but I am trying to present what you will see as a reason. If you are tricked into believing this conclusion, then I did *persuade* you, but I did not *justify* your belief (even though it is true), because your belief is based on falsehoods that are not real reasons for the conclusion that you believe. Hence persuasion is yet another purpose of arguments that is distinct from justification of beliefs or of actions.

Yet another kind·of reason is one that explains *why* something happens – it explains phenomena instead of justifying belief in those phenomena. Imagine that you visit the Fukushima nuclear power plant in Japan and see that it lies in ruins. You know that it was destroyed. You can see that. But you still wonder what destroyed it. The well-known explanation is that it was destroyed by a tsunami. This explanation can be put in a simple argument: 'This power plant was hit by a tsunami. Any power plant that is hit by a tsunami is destroyed. That is why (as well as how) this power plant was destroyed.' This argument gives you a reason why it was destroyed, even though you had already believed that it was destroyed. It *explains* the phenomenon without *justifying* belief in the phenomenon.

Is it a problem that our definition allows arguments to give any of these kinds of reasons? No, not at all. On the contrary, it is a virtue of our definition that it encompasses so many kinds of reasons, because arguments can be used to give all of these different kinds of reasons. Just as reasons can justify beliefs or actions or explain phenomena, so can arguments. Arguments can be defined as presenting reasons because the vagueness (or, more precisely, non-specificity) of the notion of reasons matches the variety in the purposes of arguments.

When is an argument (being) given?

Fine, you might think, arguments present reasons. Still, that does not yet tell us how to identify when an argument occurs. How can we tell when speakers are arguing and when they are not? We just need to figure out when they are presenting reasons. But how can we determine that?

It is often surprisingly simple, because speakers use special words to mark arguments and reasons. Imagine that someone says only this:

Marco Polo opened a trade route from Europe to China.
Countries that trade with each other affect each other.
What happened in China affected Europe.

So far, this is just a list of three sentences or propositions. We can turn it into an argument simply by adding the little word 'so'.

Marco Polo opened a trade route from Europe to China.
Countries that trade with each other affect each other.
So, what happened in China affected Europe.

The word 'so' marks this list as an argument by indicating that the first two propositions are presented as reasons for the last proposition. We can pull the same trick with other words:

Because Marco Polo opened a trade route from Europe
    to China,
and countries that trade with each other affect each other,
what happened in China affected Europe.

In this way, words like 'so' and 'because' signal that an argument is being given, so we will call them *argument markers*. Sometimes the sentence after the argument marker is the premise or reason, and we can call these words *reason markers* or *premise markers*. In other cases, the sentence after the argument marker is the conclusion, and we can call these words *conclusion markers*. In our examples, the word 'so' is a conclusion marker and the word 'because' is a reason marker. Of course, there are many more conclusion markers, including these: 'therefore', 'thus', 'hence', 'accordingly', 'which shows/establishes/proves/is evidence that', and so on. There are also many more reason markers, including these: 'since', 'for', 'which can be shown/established/proven by the fact that', and so on. All of these words and others like them indicate that an argument is in the offing.

This move is amazing. Adding one little word can miraculously turn a mere list of sentences into an argument. 'It is raining, *and* I am carrying an umbrella' is *not* an argument, but 'It is raining, *and that is why* I am carrying an umbrella' *is* an argument, as is 'It is raining, because I am carrying an umbrella.' Of course, this second argument is horrible, because my carrying an umbrella cannot explain why it is raining. Still, it is an argument, even if it is a very bad one.

It matters whether a speaker is presenting an argument, because it changes the kinds of criticism the speaker is subject to. If I say, 'Honghong is short, *which shows that* she is not a good football player', then I am offering an argument and can be criticized if the argument is bad – that is, if shortness is not a strong enough reason why someone is bad at football. In contrast, suppose I say only, 'Honghong is short, *and* she is not a good football player.' Now I merely assert both sentences, but do not claim any relation between them. I am not arguing from one to the other or claiming that one is a reason for the other. Hence I cannot be criticized if the argument is bad. That is why it matters whether a speaker is offering an argument.

Because it matters, we need to be careful. Argument markers indicate the presence of an argument – but not always. We cannot simply look at the words. We need to think about what they mean in the context. One of my favourite music albums is *Aereo-Plain* by John Hartford. One of its songs begins: 'Because of you I close my eyes each time I yodel, and so shall it be for now.' Here the word 'so' is not being used as an argument marker. If it were, then we could figure out which claim is the premise and which is the conclusion; but there is no premise or conclusion in 'so shall it be for now'. Another indication is that we cannot substitute a different argument marker; it makes no sense to say, '. . . and therefore shall it be for now'. Instead, what this clause means is simply 'that is the way it will be for now'.

What about 'because'? Here there is a conclusion: 'I close my eyes each time I yodel.' But what is the premise? The word 'you' is not a premise or a reason. Besides, we cannot substitute another argument marker; it makes no sense to say 'since of you' or 'since you'. Hence he might not be using 'because' as an argument marker either. In any case, we cannot safely assume that he is giving an argument simply because he uses the word 'because' any more than we can assume that he is giving an argument simply because he uses the word 'so'. We need to look beyond the surface form of the words and think about what those words mean and how they fit into their context in order to determine whether the speaker intends to present some kind of reason for a conclusion. One useful test, which we just saw in action, is to try to substitute other argument markers for the word that we are not sure of.

An argument can be given without any argument markers at all. Sometimes the argument marker is assumed rather than asserted. Indeed, sometimes even the conclusion is not stated openly but only suggested. For example, South Korean President Park Geun-hye was criticized for obtaining cosmetic Botox injections. One of her supporters, Kim Ku-ja, replied, 'What's so wrong about a woman getting Botox shots? Why is that a problem?'[6] Kim Ku-ja's rhetorical questions clearly suggest that she believes that there is nothing wrong at all and there is no problem with receiving Botox injections. She suggests this argument: 'There is nothing wrong with getting Botox shots. People should not criticize anyone for doing what is not wrong. So, people should not criticize Park Geun-hye for getting Botox shots.' Nonetheless, Kim Ku-ja does not actually assert any premise or conclusion. She only asks questions, and questions cannot be premises or conclusions in arguments (since they are not declarative). Hence, Kim Ku-ja does not actually assert any argument – she only indirectly suggests one.

Implied arguments like this demonstrate why we need to be careful in thinking about whether a speaker is offering an argument and also about what argument they are giving. Our definition can guide this investigation by leading us to ask whether the speakers intend to present any kind of reason, but the answer will remain unclear in some cases. When we are not sure whether a speaker intends to offer an argument, we can still ask what the argument would be and whether it would be any good. After all, what matters is whether there is a reason for the conclusion.

CHAPTER 7

How to Stop Arguments

Once arguments start, they are hard to stop. This truism does not mean that it is hard to stop a fight. We already saw that arguments are not fights. Instead, the problem here is that an argument needs premises. Why should we believe its premises? To justify the premises, we need another argument. But then that second argument also has its own premises that need to be justified by a further argument that then has premises of its own that also need to be justified by yet another argument, and so on for ever. This infinite regress lays out another way in which arguments are hard to stop after they start. It makes some sceptics wonder whether arguments can accomplish anything beyond what is already packed into their premises. This chapter will discuss some ways to address that challenge.

Can we stop soon?

To see the problem, imagine that I believe that the film *Lagaan* is about taxes and cricket in India. (It is a great film. You should watch it.) My belief is true, but is it justified? The mere fact that I believe it cannot make me justified in believing it. After all, many people believe all sorts of silly claims without any justification.[1] Moreover, the fact that my claim is true also cannot make me justified in believing it, since I might believe it for no reason or for a very silly reason. We need at least some decent justification, reason or evidence in order to be justified. One way for me to justify my belief is by watching the film so that I gain visual evidence from my own eyes. Even if I have never seen the film, I might become justified in believing my claim by reading a review that describes its plot. However, if I have never seen it and have not heard or read any reports about it, then it is hard to see how I could be justified in believing that *Lagaan* is about taxes and cricket in India.

If I do have evidence, then I can transform that evidence into the form of an argument. If my belief is based on personal experience, then my argument might be as simple as something like this: 'I watched the film *Lagaan*. I could see and hear that it was about taxes and cricket in India. I can recognize taxes, cricket and India when I see and hear about them. Therefore, *Lagaan* is about taxes and cricket in India.' Alternatively, if I did not see it but read about it, then I could argue like this: 'Wikipedia reports that *Lagaan* is about taxes and cricket in India. Wikipedia usually gets such facts right. Therefore, *Lagaan* is about taxes and cricket in India.' Either way, I am justified in believing that *Lagaan* is about taxes and cricket in India only because I have information that could be built into some argument or other (although I might not need to formulate any argument explicitly). If I do not have enough evidence for any argument of any kind, then I cannot be justified in believing that *Lagaan* is about taxes and cricket in India.

Of course, each of these arguments has premises that could be questioned. My appeal to personal experience assumes that I can tell cricket from other sports and that I did not mishear or misremember what was said in the movie. However, I need some reason to assume that I can reliably detect cricket, since *Lagaan* might be about some other sport that I have never heard of that looks a lot like cricket. I also need a reason to assume that I can tell whether the movie is about India as opposed to Pakistan, Bangladesh or Sri Lanka, for example, since the borders have changed, and I am no expert on that area of the world. Moreover, I need some reason to assume that my hearing and memory are reliable in this case, since I sometimes misunderstand what people say, and my memory is not perfect. Thus I need several reasons to back up the assumptions in my original argument. That requires other arguments with their own premises, such as that I watched the film several times, the film mentions taxes, cricket and India often, and I have made mistakes only rarely when there is repetition like this. However, these premises still could be questioned, and then they would need to be justified by yet another argument, and so on. If this regress never comes to an end, then it is hard to see how I could ever become justified in believing that *Lagaan* is about taxes and cricket in India. That result would be surprising and upsetting.

This problem generalizes to all beliefs, according to philosophical sceptics.[2] They assume that every premise needs to be justified by some evidence, that evidence can always be put into some kind of argument, that every argument needs premises, and that an argument cannot make its conclusion justified unless its premises are justified. These plausible principles together generate an infinite regress: premises need justification that needs more premises that need more justification that needs more premises that need more justification, and so on for ever. If there is no escape from this regress, then how could anyone ever be justified in believing anything?

What if we can't stop arguing?

The challenge here is to show (1) how any claim could be justified without any evidence; (2) how a claim could be justified by evidence that could not be put in the form of an argument; or else (3) how an argument could justify its conclusion by appealing to premises that are not justified themselves. Philosophers have debated for centuries about whether and, if so, how this challenge can be met. I personally doubt that this regress problem has any general theoretical solution.[3] To some extent, then, sceptics are correct that no belief is justified to the extent and in the way that they require.

So what does this prove? Some conclude that arguments can never accomplish anything at all. In my opinion, they are far too quick to jump to such a strong conclusion. Instead, I would suggest that the regress shows only that scepticism arises from requiring too much. To avoid scepticism, we just need to moderate our desires, hopes and standards.[4] We need to learn to live with what we can accomplish, even if that is not all that sceptics might have wished.

Sceptics are not satisfied by any argument unless it rules

out every contrary possibility and convinces everyone. That is why they are never satisfied. There is always some alternative that we cannot exclude. You might feel certain, for example, that you know your own name, but how can you rule out the possibility that, shortly after you were born, the hospital switched you with another baby who had a different name?[5] You might refuse to take this alternative seriously, but that refusal does nothing to show that it is false. Nonetheless, we can still accomplish a lot by ruling out the alternatives that we and our audiences are unable to take seriously.

Do we need to convince everyone? No. After all, some people are delusional, and they can reject our premises or refuse to listen to us. Fewer people than we imagine are so immovable. Nonetheless, we cannot reach everyone, and that is fine.

We can still accomplish a lot by appealing to premises that some people reject but most people accept, especially if the audience whom we are trying to reach are among those who accept our premises. Each argument needs to aim at an audience that is open to that argument in order to succeed.

To illustrate how to limit our target in political arguments, let's simplistically and artificially divide the political spectrum into thirds. The most extreme third on the left will probably question some premise in any argument for a conservative policy. In return, the most extreme third on the right will probably question some premise in any argument for a liberal policy. These extremes will be unreachable by any argument from the other side, even if they take time to listen. Despite these limitations, however, arguments can still achieve moderate goals by aiming at the third in the middle of the political spectrum.

This middle third is more willing to listen and to try to understand us, and it does not reject common-sense assumptions. One recent study[6] found that people who held extreme positions on both sides of the climate change debate updated their views only with respect to information that supported their positions and not with respect to information that conflicted. That is the bad news. The good news is that moderates in the same debate revised their views in light of information from both sides. They responded to evidence of all kinds. If this trend is repeated in other debates, then some arguments can reach this middle third by using premises that they accept, even if some extremists reject those premises. And reaching the middle third is usually enough to sway an election – if we are lucky – and then this moderate audience matters. In this way, arguments can often achieve important practical goals, even if these practical goals are limited and there is no general theoretical reply to the challenge of the sceptical regress.

How can we stop arguing?

We still need to figure out how to reach limited audiences with premises that they will not reject. In other words, we need regress stoppers for real life. Luckily our language already supplies tools for this purpose. There are four main categories of regress stoppers: guarding, assuring, evaluating and discounting. These groups of words offer different ways of handling potential objections.

GUARDING

Our first way to stop the regress is to weaken the premise. To see how this works, imagine that you own a house in a low-lying area. A visiting insurance agent argues, 'You should buy a flood insurance policy, because all houses in low-lying areas are destroyed by floods.' This argument is easy to refute, because its premise is false: it is not true that *all* houses in low-lying areas are destroyed by floods; some survive. To guard against this objection, the insurance agent can restate the premise: *some* houses in low-lying areas are destroyed by floods. Now this guarded premise is true, but the argument runs into another problem: its premise is too weak to support its conclusion. If only one house in a million in a low-lying area is destroyed by a flood, then this is not enough to justify spending money on flood insurance. What the insurance agent needs is a middle path between a premise that is too strong to defend ('all') and another premise that is too weak to support the conclusion ('some'). Here's one intermediate possibility: *many* houses in low-lying areas are destroyed by floods. This premise seems both true and strong enough to provide a reason to buy flood insurance. Of course, the term 'many' is too vague to specify how strong this reason is (which affects how much you should spend on flood insurance). Nonetheless, the move from 'all' to 'many' improves the argument by avoiding some initial objections.

The same goal can be achieved by admitting uncertainty. Instead of claiming that your house definitely will be destroyed by a flood, the insurance agent could say this: 'You should buy a flood insurance policy, because your house *might* be destroyed by a flood.' However, the fact that there is *some possibility* of a flood is hardly enough to justify buying flood insurance. If it were, then we would also have to buy meteor insurance, since any house *might* be destroyed by a meteor. A persistent insurance agent could try this premise: 'Your house has *a significant chance* of being destroyed by a flood.' The vagueness in the term 'significant' raises questions, but at least it makes the premise easier to defend and still strong enough to provide some reason for the conclusion.

These simple examples illustrate how guarding terms work. To change the premise from 'all' to 'many' (or 'most') or 'some', or from 'definitely' to 'possibly' or 'significant chance' (or 'probably' or 'likely') is to guard the premise. Other ways to guard premises include self-description, as in 'I believe (or think or suspect or fear) that your house will be destroyed by a flood', since to object to this claim about my own mental state would be to deny that the speaker believes what he says he believes. How could we deny *that*? The purpose of all such guarding terms is to make premises less vulnerable to objections and thereby to turn bad arguments into better arguments and to stop the regress of reasons.

Despite their usefulness, guarding terms can be misused. One common trick is to introduce but then drop a guarding term. An insurance agent might argue, 'A flood might destroy your house. That would be horrible. Just think of your cherished possessions. Your family could incur huge medical bills and would have to live elsewhere until you found a new home. In that case, our flood insurance policy will pay all of those expenses. Those costs add up to much more than the price of flood insurance. So flood insurance is a good deal.' What happened here? At the end, the insurance agent compares the costs of a flood destroying your house to the price of flood insurance. That comparison is relevant if your house will in fact be destroyed by a flood. However, the opening premise claimed only that a flood *might* destroy your house. If there is only a minute chance that a flood will destroy your house, then the costs of such destruction would need to be many times more than the price of flood insurance in order to make insurance worth the cost. The insurance agent has tried to hide this obvious point by dropping the guarding term. Watch out for this trick.

Another trick is to omit quantifiers entirely. People often say things like, 'Houses in low areas are destroyed by floods.' Does this mean all, some, many or most houses? If it means *all* houses, then it is false. If it means only some houses, then it is true, but not enough to support buying insurance. If it means many houses, then it is vague. Which is it? Until we know more precisely what this premise claims, we cannot determine whether the argument around it works. When someone tries to pull this trick, your best reply is usually: 'What do you mean: all, some, many or most?'

Let's apply this lesson to a controversial political example. In early 2017, the United States stopped issuing visas to people from six Muslim-majority countries: Iran, Libya, Somalia, Sudan, Syria and Yemen. Although the list of countries was modified later in 2017, let's ask what kind of argument could support the original travel ban.

One common premise is simple: Muslims are terrorists. But what exactly does this mean? This premise is too vague to assess until we specify whether it refers to all, some, many or most Muslims. The first possibility suggests this argument:

'All Muslims are terrorists. Everyone from these six countries is Muslim. Therefore, everyone from these countries is a terrorist.' This argument is obviously so bad that nobody ever presents it like this. Even the most ardent defender of the ban realizes that some people from these countries are not Muslims, and most Muslims (as well as most visa applicants) from these countries are not terrorists.

How can we fix this argument with a guarding term? One way is to weaken the premise from 'All Muslims are terrorists' to 'Some Muslims are terrorists.' This premise is easier to defend than the claim that all Muslims are terrorists. However, now it is too weak to support the conclusion. If we start the argument with 'Some Muslims are terrorists', then the premise will not be enough to support a ban on *all* people from these countries. How can we justify banning some political refugees who are not terrorists just because they happen to live in a country where some other people are terrorists? We need more justification for a ban on the whole country, so this premise has been guarded too much.

As with insurance, what we need is a middle path between a premise that is too strong to defend and one that is too weak to justify the conclusion. What about 'Many Muslims are terrorists'? Is that premise strong enough to support a ban on everyone from these countries? I do not see how. One simple reason is that, even if many Muslims are terrorists, it still might be true that no terrorists come from these six countries. So at least we need a premise like 'Many Muslims in each of these countries are terrorists.' Now, is that enough? Not yet, partly because the term 'many' is so vague. Ten thousand terrorists is many terrorists. But then, if ten million people live in a country, and ten thousand are terrorists, that means that many people in that country are terrorists even though only one in a thousand is a terrorist. If we refuse visas to everyone from that country on the grounds that 'many' are terrorists, then we ban 999 non-terrorists for every one real terrorist.

Maybe another kind of guarding term will work. It is true that every visa applicant from any of these countries *might* be a terrorist. However, it is also true that anyone from any country *might* be a terrorist. There is always some possibility, so a premise with the guarding term 'might' cannot justify a ban on these countries without also justifying a ban on all other countries. Next, defenders of the travel ban could try this premise: 'There is a significant chance (or too much chance) that any visa applicant from any of these countries is a terrorist.' However, some visa applicants have evidence that they are fleeing terrorism, so it is not clear why there is a significant chance that these particular applicants are terrorists. But then that guarded premise seems false.

Thus it is hard to see how guarding in these ways could save this argument. Indeed, the fact that this argument is so dubious should make us wonder whether this argument is what proponents of a travel ban really have in mind. If we want to make fun of them, we might put such words into their mouths. But if we really want to understand them and their position, then we need to try to look at the issue from their perspective.

What other arguments could they have in mind? One answer is suggested by asking why these six countries were singled out. It cannot be simply that they have Muslim majorities, since many other countries with Muslim majorities were not on the list. (Two non-Muslim majority countries – North Korea and Venezuela – were added to the ban later in 2017.) Instead, defenders of the ban claim that these countries' governments are weak, corrupt and chaotic, which makes it easy for terrorists to obtain false documents. Without trustworthy evidence, border officials cannot tell which visa applicants from these countries are terrorists. If even one in a thousand of those applicants are terrorists, and we have no reliable way to tell which ones they are, then it is dangerous to issue visas to any of them. Whether it is *too* dangerous is another issue, but there is surely *some* danger in issuing visas without adequate evidence of safety. If this is the problem, then there is no need to guard the premise by moving from 'all' to 'some' or 'many' or from 'definitely' to 'possibly'. The issue here is not the number of terrorists or the probability in a specific case, but the unreliability of information about which visa applicants are terrorists. That lack of trust in available evidence explains why defenders of the ban want extreme vetting in all doubtful cases, and a complete ban when the political situation makes extreme vetting insecure or impossible.

I am not, of course, saying or suggesting that this argument is good or that it is bad. Evaluation is a separate task for later chapters, and it requires detailed factual information about the particular case. Here I am merely trying to determine which argument lies behind the travel ban so that I can understand why good and reasonable people support it and so that I can appreciate their reasons, learn from them and figure out how to compromise with them. I suspect that at least some supporters of the ban have in mind something like this argument about trusting sources, but other ban supporters may have in mind very different arguments. If so, then we need to figure out what those other arguments are and then try to learn from them and work with them.

ASSURING

The issue of trust is addressed directly by a second way to head off questions and objections. Suppose that you wonder whether Sharif likes you, and I want to convince you that he does. I might say, 'I assure you that he likes you a lot.' It would be impolite or at least uncomfortable for you to reply, 'Your assurances are no good, because I do not trust you.' Thus my assurance prevents you from objecting to what I say. But notice that I did not give any particular reason or evidence for my claim that Sharif likes you. I did not say that he told me that he likes you, that I overheard him praising you or saw him acting as if he likes you, or that a mutual friend reported such things about Sharif. When I say, 'I assure you that he likes you', I suggest that I have some reason for assuring you, but I do not openly specify what that reason is. As a result, you have no particular reason to object to. I also avoid saying how strong the reason is and how trustworthy the sources are. By specifying so little, my claim or premise becomes less objectionable and easier to defend. That is how assurance stops the argument and avoids a regress.

Instead of saying, 'I assure you', I could say, 'I am sure' or 'Surely', 'I am certain' or 'Certainly', 'I have no doubt', 'Undoubtedly', 'There is no question' or 'Unquestionably', 'Obviously', 'Definitely', 'Absolutely', 'As a matter of fact', and so on. All such assuring terms suggest that there is a reason for a claim without specifying what that reason is. They thereby prevent the audience from asking for any more justification of the claim.

Assurances are perfectly fine in many cases. Some premises really are obvious, and sometimes opponents agree on certain premises as well as on the reliability of certain sources of information. It makes sense to say that evidence and experts support a claim without specifying any particular evidence or experts in situations where it would be pointless or distracting to go into more detail. Assurances can save time.

Despite these legitimate uses, assuring terms can also be misused. One common trick is *abusive assuring*. People often resort to excesses like these: 'You would have to be blind not to see that . . .', 'Everybody who knows anything knows that . . .' or (in the opposite direction) 'Only a naive fool would be deluded into imagining that . . .' Whenever people turn to abusive assurances like these, you should wonder why they adopted such desperate incivility instead of giving evidence for their claim.

Another trick is to allude to some source – authority or evidence – that you know your audience would reject, without admitting that you are relying on this dubious source. Disputed reasons cannot resolve disputes. Imagine that a liberal watches a liberal news show (such as on the American network MSNBC) and says '*Of course* the President colluded with our enemies' or 'Anybody who keeps up with the news *knows* that.' These assuring terms do not explicitly mention the particular news source, so conservative opponents cannot object to this claim by criticizing its particular source. The same point applies to a conservative who watches conservative news (such as Fox) and says, '*Only a dupe of fake news* [or the mainstream media] would accuse the President of colluding with our enemies.' When assuring terms are used on both sides to refer to news sources that opponents reject, these assuring terms silence reasons on both sides, because neither can discuss the reliability of unnamed sources. Such assuring terms stop argument, but they stop it too early.

Let's apply these lessons to the United States travel ban discussed above. Imagine a visa applicant from Somalia or Yemen who says, 'I assure you that I am not a terrorist.' An official whose job is to issue visas would have reason to doubt this assurance, since it is exactly what a terrorist would say. But then suppose an observer (perhaps another official or visa applicant) says, 'She is unquestionably only trying to escape war and terrorism.' A visa official might trust this observer, but the rules still might require reliable documentation. Even if the observer assures, 'There is plenty of evidence that this visa applicant is safe', the official would be well within his rights to ask to see that evidence. Then suppose that the visa applicant produces what looks like an official document. Now the other side can resort to assurances. The official might reply, 'That document is *clearly* unreliable. We *know* that documents like this are for sale on the streets of this country, and terrorists *undoubtedly* buy them.' These assurances give some reason for turning down the visa application, even though they do not say why the unreliability is clear or why the official knows about the sales and has no doubts that terrorists buy fake documents. That non-specificity leaves the visa applicant with no way to respond to the official's scepticism.

The problem is that assurances work only in a context of trust. If you tell me that you are certain, and if I trust you, then I might agree without needing to ask why you are certain. But if I do not trust you, then I will not be swayed by your assurance that you are confident or certain. Polarization often creates such lack of trust, so it undermines many attempts to share reasons, which breeds even more polarization.

EVALUATING

A third way to stop arguments is to use evaluative or normative language. Philosophers have wrangled for centuries about the meanings of evaluative words like 'good' and 'bad' as well as normative words like 'right' and 'wrong'. I will not try to describe or contribute to those general debates here. I will only try to show how evaluative language helps to stop arguments in much the same way as assuring.

One venerable tradition suggests that to call something good is to say that it meets the relevant standards.[7] An apple is good when it is crunchy and tasty. A car is good when it is roomy and efficient (as well as pretty, responsive, inexpensive and so on). The standards for good apples are very different from the standards for good cars, but each is good when it meets the standards that are relevant to a thing of its own kind. Similarly, to call something bad is to say that it fails to meet the relevant standards. Bad apples are mushy or bland, whereas cramped, slow gas guzzlers are bad cars.

The terms 'good' and 'bad' can apply to almost anything, but other evaluative terms are more specialized. A bargain has a good price. A beautiful painting looks good. A catchy tune has a good melody. A courageous person is good at facing danger. An honest person tells the truth when it is good to do so (but can remain silent when that is better). Such terms are evaluative, because they cannot be explained or defined adequately without referring to what is good and thereby to some relevant standards.

Speakers often use terms for evaluation even when those words are not evaluative in themselves. If I say that my child died, I surely evaluate this death as bad, but all I say explicitly is that this death occurred. I do not openly call it bad, and I can define when a death occurs without implying that the death is bad. Hence, the word 'death' is not by itself an evaluative word, even though death is bad. Similarly, to call someone liberal is not in itself an evaluative word, even though conservatives sometimes criticize their opponents by calling them liberal. Liberals are proud to be liberals, so they do not see this word as a negative evaluation. To call someone liberal is, therefore, only to describe that person's political views and is not to say that the person meets or fails to meet any evaluative or normative standards. Hence, words like 'liberal' and 'conservative' are not intrinsically evaluative.

Let's apply this point to our previous example of the United States travel ban. Its defenders will say that it is dangerous to issue visas to citizens of Iran, Libya, Somalia, Sudan, Syria and Yemen. What does it mean to call this dangerous? It seems to imply that it is too risky. But what makes it *too* risky instead of just risky? This appears to mean that it exceeds the standards of acceptable risk. The appeal to standards shows why the term 'dangerous' suggests a hidden evaluation. The same applies on the other side of this debate.

Opponents of the travel ban argue that it is safe to issue visas to some applicants from these six countries. Do they mean that this creates no risk at all? That would obviously be implausible, so it is unlikely to mean this. What they mean instead is probably that issuing these visas meets the standards of acceptable risk. It is not *too* risky. Understanding these claims in terms of relevant standards therefore clarifies the issue. The disagreement is over how much risk is created by issuing visas and how much risk is acceptable. Locating the debate in this way will not resolve it, of course, but it helps each side appreciate the other.

Now we can see how evaluative language could stop sceptical regresses. Recall that assuring terms claimed there is some reason without specifying any particular reason, thereby avoiding objections to any particular reason. Evaluation works like that. When one side of a debate calls something good, they say that it meets the relevant standards. They do not, however, specify what those standards are. Even when they use a thick term, such as when they call a policy 'safe' or 'dangerous', they locate a general kind of standard, but still do not indicate precisely what that standard dictates. This vagueness makes it harder for opponents to object, because they do not know which standards to object to. In addition, evaluative language can create alliances among people with very different standards. You and I can agree that a route to our destination is good, even if you call it good because it is short, and I call it good because it has beautiful views. You and I can agree that a fight between us would be bad, even if you call it bad because it is bad for you, and I call it bad because it is bad for me. Thus we can agree on evaluative premises in an argument, even if we accept those premises on very different standards. That agreement can obviate any need to ask for further justification of these premises, so it can provide a shared starting point for arguments.

DISCOUNTING

A fourth and final way to handle objections is to anticipate and defuse them. It might seem odd to raise new objections to your own position. Are you trying to refute yourself? However, if you state an objection and respond to it before your opponents do, then you get to formulate that objection in the way that you want instead of in the way that they would prefer. You also make your opponents reluctant to object to your premises, because their objection will seem redundant after you have already dealt with the issue. And you get to discount this objection – that is, say why you think it does not matter. This strategy can sometimes bring an end to the argument.

These functions are performed by discounting terms. Simple examples abound in everyday life. Contrast these two sentences:

(1) Ramona is smart but boring.
(2) Ramona is boring but smart.

The difference is subtle but crucial: someone who says (1) probably does *not* want to spend time with Ramona, because she is boring. In contrast, someone who says (2) probably *does* want to spend time with Ramona, because she is smart. What comes before or after the word 'but' makes all the difference.

This asymmetry arises because each of these sentences makes three claims. First, both (1) and (2) imply that Ramona is both smart and boring. In this way, 'but' resembles 'and', though it adds more. Second, discounting terms like 'but' also suggest some conflict or tension between the two claims. I can say that Ramona is strong and tall, but it sounds odd to say that Ramona is strong but tall, since there is no conflict between being strong and being tall. In contrast, there is a conflict or tension between being smart and being boring, because her being smart is a reason to spend time with Ramona, whereas her being boring is a reason not to spend time with Ramona. Third, sentences with discounting terms also indicate which side prevails in the conflict. The word 'but' suggests that the claim after 'but' is *more* important than the claim before 'but'. That is why people who say 'Ramona is smart but boring' do *not* want to spend time with Ramona, because they see her being boring as more important than her being smart. In contrast, people who say 'Ramona is boring but smart' *do* want to spend time with Ramona, because they see her being smart as more important than her being boring. This third claim explains the difference between sentences (1) and (2).

Other discounting terms make the same three claims, but in the opposite direction. Consider a political example. Dilma Rousseff was President of Brazil from 2011 until she was impeached at the end of August 2016. During July 2016, while Rousseff was still in the process of being impeached, a Brazilian might say:

(3) Although Rousseff is the President of our country, she is corrupt.

(4) Although Rousseff is corrupt, she is the President of our country.

These sentences claim that Rousseff is both President and corrupt, and they suggest some tension between those claims. Her being President is a reason to respect Rousseff, but her being corrupt is a reason not to respect Rousseff. In addition, the term 'although' usually indicates that what comes immediately after it is *less* important than the claim in the first clause. That is why someone who says (3) with the right intonation suggests that we do *not* owe respect to Rousseff, because of her corruption. In contrast, someone who says (4) with the right intonation suggests that we *do* owe respect to Rousseff, because she is the President of our country. The placement of the claims reveals the speaker's priorities.

These two patterns recur in other discounting terms, including 'though', 'even though', 'even if', 'while', 'whereas', 'however', 'yet', 'still', 'nevertheless' and 'nonetheless'. All of these terms imply both of the claims that they connect, suggest a conflict between those claims and rank those claims in importance to the issues at hand.

Arguers often use discounting terms to protect and support their premises. They might say something like, 'You should let Rousseff speak. Although her critics might object that she is corrupt, she is still President.' The second sentence responds to the critics' objection to letting her speak and also adds a premise ('she is still President') to support the conclusion that you should let her speak. Raising the objection and responding to it makes critics more reluctant to object to your premises, so it can sometimes stop an argument.

Let's apply this lesson to our continuing example of the US travel ban. Defenders of the travel ban might say, 'Sure, most Muslims from those six countries are not terrorists, but we cannot tell which ones are.' This sentence heads off the objection that the ban mistakenly assumes that most Muslims from those countries are terrorists, since defenders of the ban just explicitly denied that assumption. On the other side, opponents of the travel ban might say, 'Admittedly, we cannot always trust local documents or be sure who is a terrorist, but extreme vetting will make some cases clear.' This sentence explains why (and thereby admits that) it is difficult to tell who is a terrorist, so it heads off an imagined objection that opponents of the ban are so naive as to assume that it is easy to tell who is a terrorist. Both cases of discounting here prevent a potential misinterpretation and thereby increase the chances of mutual understanding and productive discussion. By mentioning both the objection and the response, these sentences bring to light reasons on both sides of the issue. The resulting awareness of competing considerations can increase the odds of finding a compromise that satisfies the parties and the reasons given on both sides. This is another way in which discounting objections can improve arguments.

How can words work together?

We have encountered ways to introduce arguments – argument markers – as well as ways to stop arguments – using guarding, assuring, evaluating or discounting terms. Each of these bits of language is fascinating and complex. There is a lot more to learn about them and from them. The best way to learn more is to practise identifying these words in real arguments. That is the goal of close analysis.

As an illustration, we will work slowly and carefully through one extended example. It comes from an advertisement for Equal Exchange fair trade coffee.[8] Let's begin by reading the whole advertisement in order to see its overall structure:

> It may be a little early in the morning to bring this up, but if you buy coffee from large corporations, you are inadvertently maintaining the system which keeps small farmers poor while lining the pockets of rich corporations. By choosing Equal Exchange coffee, you can help to make a change. We believe in trading directly with small farming cooperatives at mutually agreed-upon prices with a fixed minimum rate. Then, should the coffee market decline, the farmers are still guaranteed a fair price. So have a cup of Equal Exchange coffee and make a small farmer happy. Of course, your decision to buy Equal Exchange need not be completely altruistic. For we take as much pride in refining the taste of our gourmet coffees as we do in helping the farmers who produce them. For more information about Equal Exchange or to order our line of gourmet, organic and shade-grown coffee directly, call 1 800 406 8289.

To perform a close analysis of this passage, we need to identify its argument markers as well as its guarding, assuring, discounting and evaluating terms. That exercise will reveal its central arguments.

The second word is already worthy of comment. Why do the authors say, 'It *may* be a little early in the morning to bring this up' instead of 'It *is* a little early in the morning to bring this up'? Because readers might see this advertisement at any time in the day. If they see it in the evening, then it is not true that it is early in the morning. In order to avoid starting with a falsehood, the authors deploy the guarding term 'may'. Also, the fifth word, 'little', seems to guard against the objection that it is much too early. In any case, this kind of guarding is a bit unusual, because this sentence is not part of the central argument. The main point does not depend on what time of day the article is read.

The next noteworthy word is 'but'. We saw that 'but' is a paradigm discounting term. What does it discount here? That is not completely clear, but one interpretation is plausible. The rest of the sentence begins the argument, as we will see, and that argument is quite serious. It will suggest that buying the wrong kind of coffee harms needy victims. That issue is too heavy for most people to discuss while they are still waking up in the morning. Consequently, many people are likely to object to having this argument brought up while they are drinking their first cup of coffee. The term 'but' anticipates this objection and indicates that what follows is more important.

What follows is an if-then sentence, also called a conditional: 'if you buy coffee from large corporations, you are inadvertently maintaining the system which keeps small farmers poor while lining the pockets of rich corporations'. Notice that the authors do not accuse people of buying coffee from large corporations or of maintaining the system that keeps small farmers poor. After all, some readers might not drink coffee or they might already purchase fair trade coffee from Equal Exchange.

What is this conditional sentence doing? Its point comes from the word 'poor'. There is nothing wrong with maintaining a system if the system is not bad, but there is something wrong with keeping small farmers poor if it is bad to be poor. Notice that whether someone is poor does not depend only on how much currency or how many possessions they have. A person who makes a million rupees (about US$16,000) a year might be rich in areas where that is sufficient to live well, but still poor in areas where that is not sufficient to live a life that is good enough. Thus to call someone 'poor' seems to mean that they do not make or have enough to meet some minimum standards of a good life. In that sense, it is bad to be poor, so 'poor' is an evaluative term. (Of course, this does not mean that poor people are bad, but only that their levels of income and wealth are bad.) Now, if it is bad in this way to be poor, then it is bad to keep small farmers poor; and it is also bad to maintain a system with that bad effect, so it is bad to buy coffee from large corporations, if that maintains a bad system, as the sentence claims. We can see how the negative force of the evaluative term 'poor' reverberates all the way back to the very beginning of the conditional sentence in the advertisement and implies that it is bad to buy coffee from large corporations.

What about 'lining the pockets'? Is that phrase also evaluative? It is not clear, partly because it is metaphorical. There is nothing wrong with lined pockets. However, the metaphor suggests lining (or filling) pockets with money and also suggests that the money is being hidden in the linings of pockets. The reason for hiding the money is presumably that it was obtained unfairly. If this is what the metaphor suggests, then 'lining the pockets of rich corporations' also violates standards of fairness, so it is bad. This additional point thus reinforces the claim that the system stinks, so you should not maintain it by buying coffee from large corporations.

Why do the authors add the adverb 'inadvertently'? Perhaps because they do not want to accuse readers of intentionally harming poor people. Such an accusation would be hard to prove and could backfire by angering the audience and making them stop reading. The authors want to show readers how to do better without blaming them individually for the harms of the system. In addition, by calling this harm inadvertent, the authors suggest that people who buy coffee from large corporations do not know what they are doing to poor farmers, so they have something to learn by reading on.

The first conclusion then is that the current system stinks, but the main point of the advertisement is not simply to stop readers from buying coffee from large corporations. After all, they could give up coffee entirely. Instead, the authors want readers to buy their coffee from Equal Exchange. To give a reason for this, the authors need a more positive argument.

The positive argument begins with the next sentence: 'By choosing Equal Exchange coffee, you can help to make a change.' This sentence does not actually say that a change is good. Some changes might make the system worse. However, after the first sentence of the advertisement showed why the old system was bad, the authors now seem to assume that making a change is good.

This sentence still does not explicitly say that choosing Equal Exchange coffee will in fact change anything. The reason is that the phrase 'can help' contains two guarding terms. To say that people *help* to make a change is weaker than to say that they do make a change, and to say that people *can* help to make a change is weaker than to say that they do help to make a change. Weakening this premise twice makes it easier to defend. Opponents cannot object that buying coffee from Equal Exchange is not enough by itself to change the system, because the authors of the advertisement never make that unguarded claim. Yet, despite its weakness, the doubly guarded premise is enough to support the conclusion that readers should buy Equal Exchange coffee if readers want to have some chance of being part of the solution to the problems of poor coffee farmers. That chance will not be enough to satisfy some readers. Still, some possibility of a good change is better than maintaining a bad system, so this doubly guarded claim is enough reason for many readers to drink Equal Exchange coffee.

The next sentence is tricky: 'We believe in trading directly with small farming cooperatives at mutually agreed-upon prices with a fixed minimum rate.' The authors tell you what Equal Exchange believes in, but never actually assert that they do what they believe in. The term 'believe' here might be seen as a type of guarding, because it weakens the claim in order to avoid the objection that Equal Exchange does not always actually trade directly with small farming cooperatives at mutually agreed-upon prices with a fixed minimum rate. Still, the authors clearly invite readers to assume that Equal Exchange does what they believe in.

This sentence also suggests that what they believe in is good, so it is supposed to be good to trade directly with small farming cooperatives at mutually agreed-upon prices with a fixed minimum rate. However, none of the words in this sentence is explicitly evaluative. To call an action 'trade' is not to say whether it is good or bad. To say that trade is 'direct' is not to say that it is good or bad either. To say that prices are mutually agreed upon is not to evaluate the agreement as fair or good, since some mutual agreements are unfair and bad. To say that a rate has a fixed minimum is not to say that the minimum is high enough to be fair or good. The authors never explain why any of this is good. Is that a problem for the argument? Not necessarily. It is obvious that the authors see these things as good, and they might be trying to reach only audiences who share those evaluations. Maybe the authors are not addressing anyone who thinks that it is bad for prices to be mutually agreed on. If so, then the argument might reach everyone whom the authors are trying to reach.

In any case, explicit evaluation is introduced in the next sentence: 'Then, should the coffee market decline, the farmers are still guaranteed a fair price.' The term 'fair' is openly evaluative, because something is fair only if it meets evaluative standards of fairness. What about the term 'should' in this sentence? To say that someone *should* do something is normally to imply that doing it is good. Here, however, the authors are clearly not saying that the coffee market should decline. That would be bad. In this sentence, 'should the coffee market decline' instead means '*if* the coffee market declines'.

Another word in this sentence that could be marked is 'guaranteed'. To say that a fair price is *guaranteed* is to say that the farmers are assured of, or certain to get, a fair price. Who guarantees that fair price? Presumably it is Equal Exchange, since the local law does not require fixed minimum rates. Thus, if we see the Equal Exchange corporation as the author of its own advertisement, then 'guaranteed' functions as an assuring term, because the authors use it to assure readers that farmers will get a fair price. It is equivalent to saying, 'Farmers will surely get a fair price.'

Now that we understand the rest, let's return to the first word in this sentence. 'Then' is an argument marker indicating that the preceding sentence ('We belive in trading directly with small farming cooperatives at mutually agreed-upon prices with a fixed minimum rate') is a reason for the following sentence ('[If] the coffee market decline[s], the farmers are still guaranteed a fair price'). The trade and pricing practices of Equal Exchange give an explanatory reason why prices will remain stable in the face of inevitable market declines. Because of the evaluative terms in this sentence, this argument also presents a justificatory reason to buy Equal Exchange coffee, because its practices promote something good: stability in fairness.

The next sentence explicitly draws this general conclusion: 'So have a cup of Equal Exchange coffee and make a small farmer happy.' The word 'so' functions as an argument marker which indicates that what follows is a conclusion. What is strange is only that this conclusion is an imperative: 'have a cup of Equal Exchange coffee'. Imperatives are not declarative, so they cannot be true or false. That formal feature seems to rule them out as conclusions. However, this conclusion is fine if it is elliptical for 'You ought to have a cup of Equal Exchange coffee' or 'I recommend that you have a cup of Equal Exchange coffee.' The authors seem to have intended something like these expansions.

The second half of this sentence introduces a new reason: 'make a small farmer happy'. The authors did not mention happiness before. The term 'happy' is evaluative, assuming that to make people happy is to make them feel good. This positive effect of drinking Equal Exchange coffee thus complements the reasons to avoid maintaining the unfair system. Moreover, the authors drop the guarding terms and suggest that having a cup of Equal Exchange coffee will in fact make a small farmer happy. That stronger claim reaches audiences who are satisfied only if they actually do bring about a good effect and not merely if they have a chance of helping to avoid a bad effect, as the earlier argument claimed. Unfortunately, however, it raises the question of whether having a cup of Equal Exchange coffee really will make a small farmer happy. There are reasons to doubt that, but I will not go into them here.

The next sentence illustrates a common combination of assuring and guarding: 'Of course, your decision to buy Equal Exchange need not be completely altruistic.' The phrase 'of course' assures readers that what follows is true (without openly specifying any evidence that it is true, although that evidence is coming in the following sentence). What readers are assured of is, however, guarded by the complex phrase 'need not be completely'. To say that an act *is not completely* altruistic is compatible with the act being partly altruistic, so it weakens the claim that the act is completely altruistic.

Then to say that an act *need not be* completely altruistic further weakens the claim that it is completely altruistic. This doubly guarded claim is so weak that it is compatible with the decision actually not being altruistic at all, as long as it is *possible* that the decision is *partly* altruistic. Nobody could object to that, but how could it be strong enough to support any conclusion? Well, it doesn't have to, because this sentence is not part of the positive argument for drinking Equal Exchange coffee. Instead, it responds to the possible objection that the authors are asking readers to be altruistic. There is no discounting term, but there does not have to be a discounting term in every case where an objection is discounted. Here the function of discounting an objection is supposed to be clear from the context. The point of doubly guarding the claim about altruism is to discount any objection that the authors are requiring complete altruism. Even selfish bastards will have reason to drink Equal Exchange coffee.

Why? The next sentence tells us: 'For we take as much pride in refining the taste of our gourmet coffees as we do in helping the farmers who produce them.' Here the word 'for' is an argument marker. We can tell its function because we can replace it with another argument marker – 'because' – without changing the basic meaning of the sentence. To say 'For we take as much pride' is equivalent to saying '*Because* we take as much pride'. Contrast the same word in the next sentence: 'For more information about Equal Exchange . . .'. There we cannot substitute another argument marker, since it makes no sense to say '*Because* more information about Equal Exchange . . .'.

Which argument is marked by the term 'for' in the previous sentence? It is simply: 'We take as much pride in refining the taste of our gourmet coffees as we do in helping the farmers who produce them. Therefore, your decision to buy Equal Exchange need not be completely altruistic.' The doubly guarded claim is the conclusion, so its weakness makes it easier to support. Of course, refining the taste leaves open the possibility that the taste still needs much more refinement, and taking pride in refining is compatible with that pride being misplaced. Still, the authors are clearly suggesting that their coffees taste very good, and that is a reason to buy them.

Finally, we can combine the two main strands of this argument. One reason to buy Equal Exchange coffee is that doing so can help change a bad system (as well as make a small farmer happy). Another reason to buy Equal Exchange coffee is its refined gourmet taste. The two parts together are supposed to provide a reason for any reader who cares either about helping small farmers or about personally enjoying a refined gourmet taste. The people at Equal Exchange take pride in both considerations, but the argument works for readers who care about either consideration alone, that is, even if they care only about the farmers or only about the taste. The argument thus becomes stronger by broadening the range of reasons that it shows.

As usual, I am not personally endorsing this argument or its conclusion. Whether or not you are convinced to buy Equal Exchange coffee – indeed, whether or not you even like drinking coffee – the point of this exercise in close analysis is not persuasion. Instead, the goal is understanding. I tried to make this argument look as good as possible so that we can assess and learn from the best reasons for its conclusion.

My other goal was to illustrate how complex even a simple argument can be. Our close analysis revealed how much content and strategy can be uncovered by looking closely at only eight sentences and focusing on argument markers plus guarding, assuring, evaluating and discounting terms. The process of going through one example in so much detail should, I hope, provide a model to follow in using this technique on other arguments. Close analysis can be applied equally to many other arguments in many other areas. Try it on your own favourite topics. It is fun. It is even more fun to do it with friends so that you can discuss alternative interpretations.

CHAPTER 8

How to Complete Arguments

In the previous chapter, we saw how to analyse arguments by looking closely at crucial words. This technique of *close* analysis helps readers locate parts of the argument – premises and conclusions – that are given explicitly in the text. Even after such close analysis, we still need to arrange these elements of the argument into an intelligible order and then complete this structure by inserting additional premises that are assumed but not stated openly. This method is called *deep* analysis. Close and deep analysis can be combined to produce argument *reconstruction*. The goal of this chapter is to explain deep analysis and illustrate argument reconstruction. First, however, we need to define the standard of validity that will guide these methods.

Which arguments are valid?

When non-philosophers call an argument valid, they often mean simply that it is good. The word 'valid' is then used as an evaluative term. In contrast, when philosophers (including logicians) call an argument valid, they mean something entirely different that does not imply either that the argument is good or that it is bad.

The notion of validity as it is understood by philosophers concerns the relation between the premises and conclusion in an argument. An argument is valid in this technical, philosophical sense when and only when it is not possible for there to be any situation in which all of its premises are true and its conclusion is false. This definition is also equivalent to defining an argument as valid if and only if at least one of its premises is false in every possible situation where its conclusion is false. You can think about validity in either of these ways, depending on which formulation makes the most sense to you.

Either way, it is crucial that the definition is about possibility rather than actuality. Whether an argument is valid does not depend on whether its premises or conclusion actually happen to be true. All that matters is whether a certain combination – true premises and a false conclusion – is impossible (in which case the argument is valid) or possible (in which case the argument is invalid).[1]

As a result, some arguments with true premises and a true conclusion are still not valid. Consider 'All citizens of Egypt are less than a kilometre tall, all citizens of Egypt breathe air, so all animals that breathe air are less than a kilometre tall.' These premises and conclusion are all true. Nonetheless, this argument is still not valid, because it is possible for the premises to be true when the conclusion is false. Just imagine a possible world where some giraffes grow to more than a kilometre tall. This evolution is possible, and it would make the conclusion false, but both premises could still be true if citizens of Egypt remained just like they are in the actual world. This possibility is enough to show that the argument is not valid in the technical sense that philosophers adopt, despite the three truths it contains.

On the other hand, some valid arguments have false premises and a false conclusion. For example, 'All sushi chefs are women, all women play cricket, so all sushi chefs play cricket' is a silly argument, because both premises and its conclusion are false. Despite all of this falsity, it is valid in the technical sense, because it is not possible for its premises to be true when its conclusion is false. If it is false that all sushi chefs play cricket, then there must be some sushi chef who does not play cricket. That sushi chef must be either a woman or not a woman. If that sushi chef is not a woman, then the first premise ('All sushi chefs are women') is false. And if that sushi chef is a woman, then the second premise ('All women play cricket') is false, since we are assuming that she does not play cricket. There is no possibility of a combination where both premises are true and the conclusion is false. That makes the argument valid in this technical sense (even though it is a very bad argument in other ways).

In order to determine whether an argument is valid, one method is to try your best to imagine or describe a situation in which the premises are true and the conclusion is false. If you can describe a situation with this combination of truth values, then the argument is not valid. Of course, you need to be sure that your description really is coherent. You might not notice some incoherence in the description, so you need to look carefully. Still, if you can describe a situation with this combination of truth values that seems coherent after close inspection, that apparent coherence is some reason to believe that the argument is not valid. On the other hand, suppose you fail to find any coherent description of a situation with that combination of truth values. Your failure might show only your lack of imagination instead of the validity of the argument. Still, if you tried hard enough, and you could not imagine any description that makes the premises true when the conclusion is false, that is some reason to believe that the argument is valid. Trying to describe a coherent situation that combines true premises with a false conclusion is therefore a useful start in the absence of any more technical method. The best way to master this technique is to discuss cases with friends, who might be able to imagine possibilities that you have overlooked.

When is validity formal?

Some arguments are valid because of their specific words or sentences. The argument 'My pet is a tiger, so my pet is a cat' is valid, because it is not possible to be a tiger without being a cat. However, this validity is destroyed if we substitute certain other words, such as in 'My pet is a tapir, so my pet is a dog.' Thus what makes the original argument valid is the (semantic) meanings of its words – 'tiger' and 'cat'.

In contrast, other arguments are valid by virtue of their form. Consider 'My pet is either a tiger or a tapir. My pet is not a tiger. Therefore, my pet is a tapir.' If the conclusion is false (my pet is not a tapir), and the second premise is true (my pet is not a tiger), then the first premise has to be false (my pet is not either a tiger or a tapir). Thus this argument is valid. Moreover, it remains valid no matter which words are substituted for 'tiger' and 'tapir' as well as 'my pet'. This argument is also valid: 'Your pet is either a dog or a pig. Your pet is not a pig. Therefore, your pet is a dog.' So is this one: 'My country is either at war or in debt. My country is not at war. Therefore, my country is in debt.' In every case with this form, it is not possible for the conclusion to be false in circumstances where the premises are both true. Thus this argument is valid by virtue of its form. This argument form is called *denying a disjunct* (because the 'either' and 'or' propositions are called disjuncts) or *process of elimination* (because the second premise eliminates one of the alternatives in the first premise).

It is useful to remember a few other argument forms that are formally valid as well as a few that are not valid by virtue of their form but are often mistakenly thought to be valid. The variables 'x' and 'y' can be replaced by any sentence as long as the same sentence replaces the same variable wherever that variable occurs. These argument forms are valid:

Modus Ponens: If x, then y; x; so y.
Modus Tollens: If x, then y; not y; so not x.

These argument forms are invalid:

Affirming the Consequent: If x, then y; y; so x.
Denying the Antecedent: If x, then y; not x; so not y.

(These names are derived from calling the 'if' clause the antecedent and the 'then' clause the consequent in an 'if . . ., then . . .' proposition, which is also called a conditional or hypothetical.) Here are two more valid argument forms:

Hypothetical Syllogism: If x, then y; if y, then z; so, if x, then z.
Disjunctive Syllogism: Either x or y; if x, then z; if y, then z; so, z.

If you think about these argument forms and replace their variables with any sentences of your own choice, then you should be able to see which of these forms are valid and why. Formal methods (including truth tables) have been developed for showing validity by virtue of propositional form. Other methods (such as Venn diagrams, truth trees, matrices and proofs) have also been developed for showing validity by virtue of some non-propositional forms. We will not go into those details here.[2] What matters here is only to gain some initial rough feel for which arguments are valid and when their forms make them valid.

What makes arguments sound?

Even formal validity is not enough to make an argument good or valuable. Consider this argument: 'If the Amazon is the largest river in the world, then it has the largest fish in the world. The Amazon does not have the largest fish in the world. Therefore, the Amazon is not the largest river in the world.' This argument has the form *modus tollens*, so it must be formally valid. However, its conclusion is false, because the Amazon is in fact the largest river in the world. So, how can its conclusion be false when it is valid? The answer is simply that its first premise is false. The largest fish do not live in the largest river.

What makes arguments good is not only validity but soundness. A sound argument is defined as an argument that is valid and also has all true premises. This definition guarantees that every sound argument has a true conclusion. Its validity ensures that it cannot have true premises and a false conclusion. Thus the truth of its premises entails that its conclusion cannot be false. That makes soundness valuable.

What are you assuming?

These notions of validity and soundness are useful for determining when an argument depends on an assumption that it does not state explicitly. This happens often. While you and I are scheduling a business meeting in 2019, you might say,

> We should not schedule it for 3 June, because that is the last day of Ramadan.

This is all you need to say in order to move our conversation to other possible dates, if you know that we both assume that some people whom we want at the meeting will refuse to meet on the last day of Ramadan. If we add that assumption, then we get a longer argument:

> Some people whom we want at the meeting will refuse to meet on the last day of Ramadan. We ought not to schedule the meeting on a date on which some people whom we want at the meeting will refuse to meet. Therefore, we ought not to schedule the meeting on the last day of Ramadan. 3 June 2019 is the last day of Ramadan that year. Therefore, we should not schedule our meeting for 3 June 2019.

A single sentence has grown into five sentences in two stages. What could possibly justify our putting so many words into your mouth? How can we tell whether you really do assume the extra premises in the larger argument? The answer relies on validity. It is fair to ascribe these extra assumptions to you, even though you did not say them, because they are needed in order to make your argument valid. Without the implicit assumption that 'We ought not to schedule the meeting on the last day of Ramadan', it is hard to see how your explicit premise 'That [3 June] is the last day of Ramadan' gives any reason for your explicit conclusion, 'We should not schedule it [our meeting] for 3 June.' Adding the extra premise makes the argument valid, for it is not possible that both premises are true and the conclusion is false in the same situation. The new premise thereby explains why the original premise was a reason for the original conclusion.

This addition then raises the question of why we should accept the new premise. After all, even if the argument with this premise is valid, that validity by itself does nothing to show that its conclusion is true unless its premises are true. What we need is soundness, not just validity. So we need to ask: why not schedule the meeting on the last day of Ramadan?

One potential reason is that a meeting on that day would violate some religious rule. However, whether a meeting violates a religious rule depends on the kind and time of the meeting. Moreover, even if our meeting would violate a religious rule, this fact by itself would not support the conclusion that we ought not to meet on that date. Some people might accept this rule, but atheists and secular humanists would reject it, and they might be everyone in the group that is meeting. Thus this extra premise would make the argument questionable and unable to reach this audience.

We do not need to endorse any religious rule in order to agree that a meeting does not go well when nobody shows up. That is a reason why we do not want to schedule a meeting for a date when crucial people would refuse to show up. Therefore, if we know that some people whom we want at the meeting will refuse to meet on the last day of Ramadan, that gives us a reason not to schedule the meeting on that date. This reason is captured by the initial premises in the longer argument, and its premises are acceptable to a wider audience than the alternative premises that cite a religious rule. Moreover, this premise is strong enough to make the resulting argument valid, since it is not possible for its conclusion to be false when its premises are true.

These features speak in favour of the secular interpretation of this argument. It is unfair to saddle arguers with stronger assumptions when weaker assumptions would make their arguments better. The goal of filling out assumptions in arguments is not to make the arguers look silly or stupid. Instead it is to understand their point of view and learn from it. For this purpose, we need to make arguments look as good as possible, since then they teach us more. We still might end up disagreeing, but we cannot conclude that there is no good argument for a position unless we have looked at the best possible argument for that position.

All of this together explains why it is fair to ascribe the extra premises and the longer argument to someone who explicitly asserts only the shorter original sentence. Implicit premises like these are often called *suppressed*, perhaps because the arguer supposedly suppresses an inclination to assert them openly. In general, we should ascribe suppressed premises to an arguer only if they are necessary to make the original argument valid, and only if the arguer would view the added premises as true and hence the longer argument as sound. In this way, validity and soundness are essential standards for completing arguments by adding suppressed premises.

To call a premise suppressed might seem to disparage it as sneaky. However, the term 'suppressed' here is not a negative evaluation. Everyone suppresses premises, and it is hard to see how we could (or why we would) avoid doing it. It is often legitimate for arguers to suppress premises. Indeed, it is often bad *not* to suppress premises. Just look at how much longer our completed argument is than the original sentence. If we had to spell out every assumption whenever we gave any argument, then it would take a very long time to say much at all. Suppressing premises promotes efficiency in communication.

Other arguers use this defensible tool for nefarious purposes. They try to fool fools by suppressing the most dubious premises in their arguments. Imagine a used-car dealer who argues, 'You should purchase five years of service from my dealership, because then you will not need to pay for repairs.' He is suppressing the premise that you should buy whatever will avoid repair expenses. He never comes out and asserts that extra premise, because you could question it if he did. Nonetheless, he still does need that premise in order to make his argument valid. The problem is that this suppressed premise raises crucial issues that the dealer is trying to hide. How much does the service contract cost? How likely is the car to need repairs? How expensive will the repairs be? And, of course, why is he selling you a car that is so likely to need such expensive repairs? His trick is to steer you away from those questions by focusing your attention on other premises instead of the questionable one. To avoid getting fooled by such tricks, it is useful to fill out all of the suppressed premises in an argument. That exercise will make you less likely to overlook a dubious premise that the arguer is hiding.

Do these methods scale up?

An extended example can illustrate how close analysis and deep analysis work together in argument reconstruction. Here is one example from the opening of an unsigned article entitled 'New Approaches Needed to Address Rise of Poor Urban Villages in the Pacific':

> New approaches are needed to address the challenge of rising urban dwellers in the Pacific who live in poor-quality housing with inadequate provision for basic services in settlements known as 'urban villages', a new Asian Development Bank (ADB) report says. 'There has been a rapid rise of urban villages in recent years due to increased poverty and the negative impacts of climate change,' said Robert Jauncey, head of ADB's Pacific Subregional Office in Suva, Fiji. 'These informal or unplanned settlements are often neglected and excluded from the government's planning system, so we need to rethink approaches to urban management and development to include urban villages in the mainstream policies, strategies, projects, and programs.'
>
> The report, entitled *The Emergence of Pacific Urban Villages – Urbanization Trends in the Pacific Islands*, defines urban villages as native and traditional communities and village-like settlements in urban areas that display common characteristics: association with certain ethnic groups,

strong socio-cultural ties, land tenure based on custom, heavy reliance on the informal economy, and persistence of subsistence activities. Urban village dwellers often live in hardship and poverty, and are stereotyped with negative traits . . .[3]

What we need to determine is whether this passage includes an argument, where that argument is located in the passage, what it is, what purpose it serves and how it is structured. Those tasks require careful attention to detail. We will work backwards through the text.

WITHOUT ARGUMENT

Consider the second paragraph first. Does that paragraph give any argument? No. It gives the title of the report, perhaps so that readers can look it up. Then it defines what an urban village is, presumably so readers will know what the article is about. Then it describes the lives of urban villagers. The evaluative words in this paragraph might make readers think of an argument: Urban villagers face 'hardship and poverty' as well as 'negative' stereotypes. Therefore, someone needs to help them. That argument seems implicit. However, the paragraph does not explicitly give that argument or any other. We can tell this by applying our definition of argument and looking for argument markers. Just ask where the premise and conclusion are.

JUSTIFICATION

Next consider the last sentence of the first paragraph. The argument marker 'so' indicates that an argument does occur in this sentence. However, this argument is quoted from Jauncey, so the author of the article does not assert this argument. Jauncey does. Perhaps the author of the article wants to preserve neutrality as a news reporter. Or maybe the author agreed with Jauncey. After all, the article never suggests any doubts about what Jauncey (or the ADB) has said. In any case, we can see that at least Jauncey is giving an argument, so let's try to reconstruct it.

The word 'so' is a conclusion marker that tells readers that what comes before is a reason for what follows:

> Urban villages are often neglected and excluded from government planning.
> Therefore, we need to rethink approaches to urban management and development to include urban villages in the mainstream policies, strategies, projects and programs.

The last instance of the little word 'to' is also an argument marker if it can be interpreted as 'in order to', which is plausible. This reason marker indicates that what follows it is a reason for what comes before, so we might reconstruct the whole argument like this:

> We need to include urban villages in the mainstream policies, strategies, projects and programs.
> Urban villages are often neglected and excluded from government planning.
> Therefore, we need to rethink approaches to urban management and development.

Now we have two premises and one conclusion.

What is the purpose of this argument? It is often hard to

tell precisely what someone intends, and arguers are no exception. Still, Jauncey seems to have been trying to persuade or convince his audience that his conclusion is true – that we need to rethink urban management in certain ways. He presumably believed that many in his audience did not have that belief before he spoke. They thought that urban management was going fine, at least in this area, or they did not think about it at all. So, he was trying to change their beliefs. But that is not all, we can assume. He probably also wanted them to believe his conclusion not arbitrarily but on the basis of reason. That is why he did not simply assert the conclusion, but instead presented an argument that gave reasons for the conclusion. Hence, he was trying not only to persuade but also to justify his audience's belief in his conclusion.

To see how this argument is supposed to serve that purpose, we need to fit these premises and conclusion into a structure that shows how they work together to justify the conclusion. The presence of two argument markers might seem to suggest that each premise provides a separate reason for the conclusion. On that interpretation, there are two distinct arguments:

> Urban villages are often neglected and excluded from government planning.
> Therefore, we need to rethink approaches to urban management and development.

> We need to include urban villages in the mainstream policies, strategies, projects and programs.
> Therefore, we need to rethink approaches to urban management and development.

Each of these arguments needs a suppressed premise to make it valid. In particular, the first argument needs a suppressed premise like this: 'We need to rethink any approach to urban management that neglects and excludes urban villages.' But that suppressed premise is close to the explicit premise in the second argument: 'We need to include urban villages in the mainstream policies, strategies, projects and programs.' Similarly, the second argument needs a suppressed premise something like this: 'Current approaches to urban management and development do not already include urban villages.' But that suppressed premise is close to the explicit premise of the first argument. This search for suppressed premises thus reveals that the two premises are supposed to work together (not separately) to justify the conclusion. Each depends on the other. This structure can be called *joint*.

In order to see how these premises work together, first we need to clarify the terms. In particular, the first premise refers to 'government planning', the second premise instead mentions 'mainstream policies, strategies, projects and programs', and the conclusion says 'approaches to urban management and development'. Writers often vary their wording in inessential ways to avoid the appearance of repetition. However, such unimportant variations can obscure the structure of the argument. If these three phrases describe different things, then it is hard to see how a premise about one could adequately support a conclusion about another. Then the argument would make no sense. In order to show how the argument works, then, we need to relate these phrases somehow. One option is to add a premise that identifies them: 'Mainstream policies, strategies, projects and programs as well as urban management and development are government planning.' This sentence might seem true, but it is verbose. For simplicity, I will instead replace them all with a single phrase:

> We need to include urban villages in urban management.
> Urban villages are often neglected and excluded from urban management.
> Therefore, we need to rethink urban management.

This simple rewording seems to capture what Jauncey had in mind while also revealing the relation between the premises and the conclusion.

A similar issue arises with 'include' in the first premise and 'neglected and excluded' in the second premise. Presumably what is neglected and excluded is not included, so we can slightly reword the argument again:

> We need to include urban villages in urban management.
> Urban villages are often not included in urban management.
> Therefore, we need to rethink urban management.

Uniform wording makes it clear that the different parts of this argument are about the same topic.

Next, notice the guarding term 'often'. Why does the premise say 'Urban villages are often not included in urban management' instead of simply 'Urban villages are not included in urban management'? Presumably because the latter could be read as 'Urban villages are never included in urban management', which is false. There are a few exceptions. The guarding term 'often' is needed to make this premise defensible. But does it make the premise too weak to support the conclusion? No. If half of urban management neglects urban villages, then we need to rethink that half, even if the other half is just fine. Why? Because we always need to include *all* urban villages in urban management. Including half or even 80 per cent is not enough (at least for people who live in parts that are excluded). Maybe we should add 'all' to the first premise to make this clear. After that addition, the guarding term 'often' in the second premise seems just fine.

A subtler guarding term is 'rethink'. Is Jauncey really arguing only that we need to think again or more about urban management? To answer this question, just ask: what if we rethought urban management, but still did nothing to change urban management or to help urban villages? Would Jauncey be satisfied? I doubt it. If not, then he really wants to argue not only that we need to *rethink* urban management, but also that we need to *change* urban management so as to include all urban villages. In that case, his argument really amounts to this:

> We need to include all urban villages in urban management.
> Urban villages are often not included in urban management.
> Therefore, we need to change urban management so as to
>   include all urban villages.

In contrast with the first guarding term, we had to remove this second guarding term in order to capture the real force of what Jauncey meant to say.

This argument is looking pretty good so far, but it is not really any good unless its premises are true or at least justified. In particular, what justifies the first premise? Why do we need to include all urban villages in urban management?

Jauncey does not answer that question in this sentence. However, he does work for the ADB, so it would not be surprising if he builds his argument on top of their claims.

The ADB report is quoted in the first sentence of the extract: 'New approaches are needed to address the challenge of rising urban dwellers in the Pacific who live in poor-quality housing with inadequate provision for basic services in settlements known as "urban villages".' All this sentence says openly is that new approaches are needed, and that the housing quality is poor and the basic services are inadequate. It never explicitly connects these claims by saying that one is a reason for the other. Nonetheless, the fact that the ADB evaluates the housing as 'poor' and the basic services as 'inadequate' suggests an argument:

> New approaches are needed to address the challenge of rising urban dwellers in the Pacific *because they* live in poor-quality housing with inadequate provision for basic services.

The only difference is that this revised sentence contains the argument marker 'because they' where the original sentence contained 'who'. That small difference matters. The original sentence did not openly argue from one claim to the other or say that one is a reason for the other. This new sentence says precisely that. As a result, the new sentence gives an argument even though the original did not.

Which sentence did the author really mean or intend? That is hard to tell. The context suggests that the author intends to give 'poor' and 'inadequate' as reasons why we need new approaches. Still, we cannot be sure what the author intended, because he or she did, after all, choose to write 'who' instead of 'because they'. In the face of this uncertainty, what can we do? We might try to ask the author, but the article is unsigned; and, even if we knew who the author was, he or she might be unreachable. The most constructive approach is probably to forget about what the author really meant and simply ask whether the argument that is suggested is any good. After all, we do not really care about catching this author in a mistake, as if we were scoring points in a debate. What really matters is whether we need to adopt new approaches to planning urban villages. If the argument works, then we do need a new approach to urban villages, and the argument tells us why – regardless of whether this author or anyone really meant to offer that argument.

So, let's assume that the ADB (and perhaps also the author) intended to argue something like this:

> Urban villagers live in poor-quality housing with
> inadequate provision for basic services.
> Therefore, we need new approaches to address the
> challenge of rising urban dwellers in the Pacific.

Unfortunately, this argument is hardly valid. One reason is that its premise does not mention current approaches to urban management. What if current approaches work fine and we just need to give them a little time to succeed? In that case, the premise would be true, but the conclusion would be false, because we would not need new approaches.

In order to avoid this problem, we need to add something about what is wrong with current approaches. Recall that the quotation from Jauncey in the third sentence did specify something wrong with current approaches, namely, that they often do not include urban villages. So it might help to combine these arguments, but how? One possibility is that the premise in the first sentence provides a reason for the premise in the third sentence. This relation is not obvious, because these claims are never juxtaposed, and no argument marker indicates their relation. Nonetheless, the suggestion does make sense of the argument and supports this interpretation:

> Urban villagers live in poor-quality housing with inadequate provision for basic services.
> Therefore, we need to include all urban villages in urban management.
> Urban villages are often not included in urban management.
> Therefore, we need to change urban management so as to include all urban villages.

This double argument – with two instances of the argument marker 'therefore' – uses the conclusion of the first part as a premise in the second part. The two parts form a line pointing to the final conclusion. This kind of structure is often described as *linear*.

We are still not finished, because the first argument is not valid. It is possible that urban villagers live in poor-quality housing with inadequate services, but we still do not need to include *all* urban villages in urban management. This combination could happen if their housing and services could be improved without including them in urban management. It also could happen if including them in urban management would do no good to improve their housing and services. Thus the argument will be invalid until we add some suppressed premise about a relation between urban management and the quality of housing and services. Here's a possibility:

1. Urban villagers live in poor-quality housing with inadequate provision for basic services.
2. All areas with people who live in poor-quality housing with inadequate provision for basic services need to be included in urban management.
3. Therefore, we need to include all urban villages in urban management.
4. Urban villages are often not included in urban management.
5. Therefore, we need to change urban management so as to include all urban villages.

This argument is (close enough to being) valid and presents a plausible line of reasoning.

Now we have finally arrived at a fair reconstruction of Jauncey's argument. Of course, to say that this is his argument is not to endorse it, much less to claim that its conclusion is true. The reconstruction reveals several premises that could be questioned. Critics could deny premise (1) and claim that housing and basic services really are adequate in urban villages. Maybe these urban villages are not as bad as Jauncey claims. Critics also might deny premise (4) and claim that urban management plans almost always already include urban villages. Maybe these programmes are not as bad as Jauncey claims. Finally, critics could deny premise (2) and claim that we should exclude some poor areas from urban management, either because it would be too expensive to include them or because they will be better off if they learn to fend for themselves. To respond to such critics, Jauncey would need to add more arguments, so the reconstruction hardly settles the issue in its present form. What it does instead is to clarify where critics can target their objections and where Jauncey needs arguments to back up his premises. In those ways, reconstruction helps us understand Jauncey and the issues that he raises. That is all that it can hope to do, but that is a lot more than we could accomplish without reconstructing his argument.

EXPLANATION

By moving from the third sentence to the first, we skipped the second. Did we miss part of the argument? Or does the second sentence present a different argument? Or more than one argument? I will suggest that this short second sentence actually gives two other arguments of a new kind with a new conclusion. To see why, we need to reconstruct the arguments in this second sentence.

The second sentence says, 'There has been a rapid rise of urban villages in recent years due to increased poverty and the negative impacts of climate change.' The reason marker 'due to' signals that what follows are premises in an argument for what came before:

> There has been increased poverty . . .
> There have been increased . . . negative impacts of climate change.
> Thus, there has been a rapid rise of urban villages in recent years.

This argument needs to be spelled out in much more detail, but let's start by asking what purpose this argument is supposed to serve.

Jauncey might again want to persuade his readers to believe his conclusion. However, it is hard to see how this argument would accomplish that goal. It is also hard to see why he would need to convince his readers of this conclusion, since most of them probably already know that the number of urban villages has risen rapidly in recent years. Observations make that clear. So, assuming that Jauncey knows what he is doing (and otherwise, why pay attention?), he must be seeking some other goal.

What would that be? Well, even if you know *that* urban villages have arisen, you still might wonder *why* they have arisen. Why are so many people moving so quickly into poor-quality housing with inadequate basic services? This question is what this argument seeks to answer. The answer is increased poverty and climate change. Because so many more people have become poor and have been displaced by climate change, they are willing to move into bad housing with bad services. They have no option. This explanation helps us understand why this trend is occurring by pointing to its cause. So this argument seems to be aimed at explanation instead of persuasion or justification.

If that is its purpose, what is the argument? As before, the argument has two premises, so we need to ask whether they work together in a joint structure or instead should be seen as independent explanations for the conclusion. If they are independent, then we really have two arguments:

There has been increased poverty . . .
Thus, there has been a rapid rise of urban villages in
recent years.

There have been increased . . . negative impacts of climate
change.
Thus, there has been a rapid rise of urban villages in
recent years.

When we split the argument in the third sentence above, we
saw that the two premises worked jointly, because each separate argument assumed a suppressed premise close to the
explicit premise in the other argument. That is not the case
here. Each of these two arguments is invalid, so each does indeed
assume a suppressed premise. However, neither assumes the
premise in the other argument. To that extent, these arguments work independently: one explanation is poverty, and
the other is climate change. This structure is sometimes described as *branching*.

Starting with the poverty argument, what suppressed premise is needed to make it valid? The story was already mentioned
above: when people become poor, they have no better option
than to move into bad housing with bad services, so they are
willing to put up with life in urban villages. With a few additions, we can build this explanation into an argument like this:

Poverty has increased rapidly in recent years.
As poverty increases, there are more poor people who are
willing to live in bad housing with bad services
[*suppressed premise*].

Therefore, there has been a rapid rise in recent years of poor people who are willing to live in bad housing with bad services.

As more people become willing to live in bad housing with bad services, urban villages increase in size and number [*suppressed premise*].

Therefore, there has been a rapid rise of urban villages in recent years.

This reconstruction puts quite a few words into Jauncey's mouth, but some additions like these are needed to make each part of this argument valid. They are also supposed to capture his story about how poverty explains the rise in urban villages.

The climate argument works similarly, but needs to be clarified in one way. The premise refers to 'negative impacts' of climate change without specifying which negative impacts matter. In particular, climate change is likely to kill many people. However, deaths cannot by themselves lead to urban villages, since people living in urban villages are alive, of course. What creates urban villages is displacement. When some people are killed by storms due to climate change, other people then leave the areas that were destroyed by the storms, perhaps in order to avoid being killed themselves or perhaps because their old housing was destroyed by the storms that killed others. These movements of people to avoid the effects of climate change are what Jauncey probably meant to cite as an explanation of urban villages. If so, this branch of the argument can be reconstructed like this:

Climate change has increased rapidly in recent years.

As climate change increases, many people are displaced [*suppressed premise*].

Therefore, many people have been displaced rapidly in recent years.

As more people are displaced, urban villages increase in size and number [*suppressed premise*].

Therefore, there has been a rapid rise of urban villages in recent years.

This argument is valid, but would not be valid without the suppressed premises, and Jauncey would presumably accept those suppressed premises. Thus this reconstruction is a fair representation of what he probably had in mind.

The conclusion of the climate argument is the same as in the poverty argument, so one could say that the two arguments work together to give a more complete explanation of the rate at which urban villages are rising. Urban villages increase even more rapidly when both poverty and climate change lead more people to move into urban villages. Nonetheless, each reason by itself could be seen as adequate to explain why the rise of urban villages has been rapid, even if together they explain why it has been so very rapid.

As before, to reconstruct Jauncey's argument is not to endorse it. Even though we are trying to make it look as good as possible, our reconstruction actually specifies which premises critics could attack or question. Are poverty and climate change really increasing so fast? Do poverty and climate change really displace people and lower their expectations? Do these effects cause poor people to move into urban villages?

Jauncey might or might not be able to answer such questions. If not, critics might reject his argument and his conclusion.

Reconstruction does not always lead to a good argument. Indeed, sometimes it is not possible to reconstruct an argument in any way that makes it look any good at all. Nonetheless, even in such cases, reconstructing an argument can still help us understand it. This method can also show us how to determine whether or not it is good as well as how good it is. In that way, reconstruction paves the path to evaluation, which is the topic of the next chapter.

CHAPTER 9

How to Evaluate Arguments

After we identify an argument, along with its purpose and structure, and fill it out with suppressed premises, we finally reach the point when we can evaluate it – that is, ask whether it is any good. To call something good, as we have seen, is to say that it meets the relevant standards. So, what are the relevant standards for arguments?

One standard is pragmatic. Just as we call an advertisement good when it increases sales, because that is its purpose, so we call an argument good when it serves its intended purpose. If an argument is presented in order to persuade some audience, then it is good in this pragmatic way to the extent that it succeeds in persuading that audience. However, the argument might persuade only by tricking its audience into believing something that they have no real reason to believe. The argument might offer no reason at all or only a very bad reason. In this case it persuades without justifying.

If we seek justification, understanding and truth instead of persuasion alone, then we hold arguments to a higher standard. We want arguments that provide good and adequate reasons or at least some real reason as opposed to a trick or misdirection. But then we need standards for determining when reasons are good in some epistemic sense that has to do with truth and justification instead of only belief or persuasion. That is the kind of standard and value that we will discuss in this chapter.

The particular relation to truth and justification that an arguer claims in an argument depends in part on its form. Some arguers want their premises to guarantee their conclusions, whereas others are happy with some evidence short of any guarantee. On this basis, it is common to distinguish deductive from inductive forms of arguments, so we will follow that tradition, although we will see that this distinction is problematic in some ways.

Was Sherlock Holmes a master of deduction?

Let's start with a few simple examples. Imagine someone who argues like this:

(I) Noel is a Brazilian.
     Therefore, Noel speaks Portuguese.

This argument is clearly not valid, because Noel could easily be a Brazilian who does not speak Portuguese. Maybe Noel is a baby who is too young to speak any language or a recent immigrant who has not yet learned Portuguese.

Despite these weaknesses, it is easy to add a single suppressed premise that makes this argument valid:

(II) All Brazilians speak Portuguese.
      Noel is a Brazilian.
      Therefore, Noel speaks Portuguese.

Now, it is not possible for both premises to be true when the conclusion is false. If the conclusion is false, because Noel does not speak Portuguese, then either Noel is not a Brazilian (in which case the second premise is false) or Noel is a Brazilian who does not speak Portuguese (in which case the first premise is false). This relation between its premises and conclusion makes argument (II) valid.

Great, so it is valid! Does that make argument (II) any better than argument (I)? No. Adding the suppressed premise that turned invalid (I) into valid (II) simply shifted any doubts from the relation between the premise and conclusion in (I) to the first premise in (II). This shift merely raises the question of whether we should accept that added premise.

What kind of evidence could support the premise that all Brazilians speak Portuguese? Maybe the speaker generalized from the Brazilians whom he knows. Then his argument might seem like this:

(III) All Brazilians whom I know speak Portuguese.
       Noel is a Brazilian.
       Therefore, Noel speaks Portuguese.

Unfortunately, now the argument is back to being invalid, because it is possible that I do not know Noel, who does not speak Portuguese even though he is a Brazilian.

Another possibility is that the arguer read on Wikipedia that Brazilians speak Portuguese, and he assumed this meant all Brazilians.

(IV) Wikipedia says that Brazilians speak Portuguese.
       Therefore, all Brazilians speak Portuguese.

Noel is a Brazilian.

Therefore, Noel speaks Portuguese.

The last three lines are just like argument (II), so that second part is still valid. However, the inference from the first line to the second line is clearly not valid, because Wikipedia might be wrong or might have been referring only to Brazilians in general rather than to every single Brazilian, including babies and recent immigrants.

This sequence of arguments teaches an important lesson. Argument (II) – repeated in lines 2–4 of (IV) – is the only one that is valid. By squeezing the argument into this stilted form, the speaker suggests that he intends argument (II) to be valid. After all, it is obviously valid, and it took effort to formulate it to be valid, so the speaker must have wanted it to be valid and to appear valid. In contrast, arguments (I), (III) and the first two lines of (IV) are all obviously invalid, so speakers would not formulate these arguments in this way if they intended their arguments to be valid. This contrast shows that some speakers intend their arguments to be valid, while others do not.

That intention is the difference between deductive and inductive arguments. An argument is deductive if its proponent intends it to be valid. An argument is inductive if its proponent does not intend it to be valid. Thus argument (II) is deductive, but arguments (I) and (III) are inductive. Argument (IV) combines an inductive argument in its first two lines with a deductive argument in its lines 2–4.

It might seem odd to distinguish forms of arguments in terms of what their proponents intend. The reference to intention is needed, however, because of bad deductive arguments, like this:

(V)   All Brazilians speak Portuguese.

       All citizens of Portugal speak Portuguese.

       Therefore, all Brazilians are citizens of Portugal.

If speakers were ever confused enough to give this invalid argument, then the fact that they put it in this form would suggest that they intended it to be valid. That intention explains why we would classify this argument as deductive, even though it is invalid and fallacious.

This way of distinguishing deduction and induction shows why that distinction is important. Since deductive arguments are intended to be valid, it is fair to criticize them for being invalid. In contrast, the fact that an inductive argument is invalid is no criticism at all, because it is not intended to be valid. To criticize an inductive argument for being invalid is just as inappropriate as criticizing a rugby ball for failing as a football (or soccer ball) when the rugby ball was never intended for use in that other game.

Although this notion of induction is common among philosophers and logicians, others conceive of induction very differently. Some people say that induction rises from particulars to generalizations. This characterization is inaccurate, because some inductive arguments run in the reverse direction, as we will see.

Another potential source of confusion is Sir Arthur Conan Doyle, who described his fictional detective Sherlock Holmes as a master of the science of deduction, because Holmes could draw conclusions from minor observations that others overlooked. In one story, Holmes glimpses a man on the street and immediately pegs him as 'an old soldier . . . served in India . . . Royal Artillery'. How could he tell so much so quickly? '"Surely," answered Holmes, "it is not hard to say that a man with that bearing, expression of authority, and sun-baked skin, is a soldier, is more than a private, and is not long from India . . . He had not the cavalry stride, yet he wore his hat on one side, as is shown by the lighter skin on that side of his brow. His weight is against his being a sapper [a soldier who works on fortifications]. He is in the artillery."'[1] These inferences are amazing, but are they deductive? Well, the arguments are clearly not valid, because it is possible that the man is an actor playing the part of an old artilleryman in India. Since their invalidity is so obvious, it is unlikely that anyone as smart as Holmes would have intended them to be valid. So these arguments are not deductive by our definition. That does not mean that the arguments are no good. Their brilliance is the point of the incident in the story. Still, instead of being a master of deduction, Holmes is a master of induction – in the philosophical sense of these terms.

What's so great about deduction?

Why did Conan Doyle misleadingly describe Sherlock Holmes as a master of deduction instead of induction? Perhaps to heap the highest possible praise on Holmes's reasoning. Many people assume that deduction is somehow better than induction. The comparisons among arguments (I)–(V) should already make us sceptical of this assumption, but it is worth asking why so many people believe it.

One reason for preferring deduction might be that it seems to achieve certainty by ruling out all contrary possibilities. A valid argument excludes any possibility of a false conclusion when its premises are true. Another apparent advantage of deduction is that validity is indefeasible in the sense that, if an argument is valid, then adding an extra premise can never make it invalid. (Just try it with argument (II).) Addition cannot invalidate validity.

These features of deduction seem desirable if you want certainty. Unfortunately, you can't always get what you want, according to philosophers Mick Jagger and Keith Richards. The appearance of certainty in deductive arguments is an illusion. The conclusion of a valid argument is guaranteed only if its premises are true. If its premises are not true, then a valid argument shows nothing. Hence, when we cannot be certain of its premises, a deductively valid argument cannot create certainty about its conclusion.

An argument's validity does rule out the option of believing the premises and denying the conclusion, but you still have several alternatives: you can either accept the conclusion or deny a premise. In argument (II) above, you can deny the conclusion that Noel speaks Portuguese as long as you give up either the premise that Noel is a Brazilian or the other premise, that all Brazilians speak Portuguese. The argument cannot tell you whether its own premises are true, so it cannot force you to accept its conclusion as long as you are willing to give up one of its premises.

This point is ossified in the adage: 'One person's *modus ponens* is another person's *modus tollens*.' Recall that *modus ponens* is the argument form 'If *x*, then *y*; *x*; so *y*', whereas *modus tollens* is the argument form 'If x, then y; not y; so not x.' In *modus ponens*, the antecedent x is accepted, so the consequent y is also accepted. But in *modus tollens*, the consequent y is rejected, so the antecedent x is also rejected. The conditional 'If x, then y' cannot tell us whether to accept its antecedent x and then apply *modus ponens*, or instead to deny its consequent y and then apply *modus tollens*. Similarly, a valid argument cannot tell us whether to accept its premises and then accept its conclusion, or instead to reject its conclusion and then also reject one or all of its premises. As a result, the valid argument by itself cannot tell us whether or not to believe its conclusion.

We cannot easily give up either premise if both premises are justified. However, all that shows is that the real force of a valid argument comes not from its validity but from the justifications for its premises. If my only reason to believe that all Brazilians speak Portuguese is that all Brazilians whom I know speak Portuguese, then it is hard to see why valid argument (II) is any better than invalid argument (III). The only real difference is that the uncertainty in argument (II) is about its first premise, whereas the uncertainty in argument (III) is about the relation of its premises to its conclusion. Neither form of argument avoids uncertainty. They simply locate that uncertainty in different places.

For these reasons, we need to give up our quest for certainty.[2] One way to curtail this impossible dream is to turn from deductive arguments to inductive arguments. Inductive arguments are not intended to be valid or certain. They do not try or pretend to rule out every contrary possibility. They admit to being defeasible in the sense that further information or premises can turn a strong inductive argument into a weak one. All of this might seem disappointing, but it is actually invigorating. The realization that more information could make a difference motivates further inquiry. A recognition of uncertainty also brings humility and openness to contrary evidence and competing positions. These are advantages of inductive arguments.

How strong are you?

Since inductive arguments by definition do not aim at validity, what do they aim at? The answer is strength. An inductive argument is better if its premises provide stronger reasons for its conclusion. Satisfied? I hope not. You should be asking, 'But what is strength? It is a relation between premises and conclusion, but how can we tell when one reason or argument is stronger than another? And what makes it stronger?'

No answer has achieved consensus. The notion of inductive strength is still highly controversial, but one natural way to think about strength is as probability. On this view, the strength of an inductive argument is (or depends on) the conditional probability of its conclusion, given its premises. An inductive argument is stronger when the probability of its conclusion – given its premises – is higher.

To understand this standard of strength, we need to learn a little about conditional probability. Imagine an area of India where it rains one out of five days in general, but it rains four out of five days during monsoon season. What is the probability that it will rain there on Gandhi's birthday?

That depends on the date of Gandhi's birth. If you have no idea when Gandhi's birthday is, it is reasonable to estimate this probability as one out of five or 0.20. But suppose you discover that Gandhi's birthday is during the monsoon season in this area of India. With that extra information, it now becomes reasonable to estimate the probability of rain on Gandhi's birthday as four out of five or 0.80. This new figure is the conditional probability of rain on Gandhi's birthday in this area, given that his birthday is during the monsoon season in that area.

The application to inductive arguments is straightforward. Consider this argument:

> Our parade will occur on Gandhi's birthday in that area.
> Therefore, it will rain on our parade.

This argument is neither valid nor deductive, so it makes sense to evaluate it by the inductive standard of strength. The premise by itself gives no information about when Gandhi's birthday is, so the conditional probability of the conclusion, given the premise, is 0.20. That argument is not very strong since it is more likely than not that it won't rain in that area then, given only the information in the premise. But now let's add a new premise:

> Our parade will occur on Gandhi's birthday in that area.
> Gandhi's birthday is during monsoon season in that area.
> Therefore, it will rain on our parade.

The argument is still not valid, but it is stronger, because the conditional probability of the conclusion, given the premise, has risen to 0.80. The extra information in the new premise increases the probability. All of this is common sense. If you do not know when Gandhi's birthday is, the first argument is not a strong reason to reschedule the parade. But when someone adds, 'That's during monsoon season!', then it makes sense to reschedule the parade, unless you like walking in the rain.[3]

How do I induce thee?
Let me count the ways

What is in the grab-bag of inductive arguments? Let's reach deep into the bag and see what comes out.

Imagine that you want to open a restaurant, and you have chosen a location in Edinburgh, but you have not yet decided whether to serve Ethiopian food or Turkish food, your chef's two specialties. The success of the restaurant depends on how many people in the neighbourhood like each kind of food. To answer this crucial question, you ask random people in the neighbourhood and discover that 60 per cent like Turkish food, but only 30 per cent like Ethiopian food. You conclude that these same percentages hold throughout the whole neighbourhood. This inference is a *statistical generalization* that argues from premises about the small sample that you tested to a conclusion about a larger group. Such generalizations are inductive arguments because they are not intended to be valid. The tested sample clearly might not match the whole neighbourhood.

Next, you need to test items for your menu. You decide to try them out on friends and neighbours, but you do not want to test Turkish food on people who do not like it, since they won't come to your restaurant anyway. You wonder whether your neighbour to the south of your restaurant likes Turkish food. You don't know anything special about him, so you conclude that he has a 60 per cent chance of liking Turkish food. This argument can be called a *statistical application*, because it applies a generalization about the whole population to an individual. It is inductive, because it is clearly not valid. It could underestimate the probability if, for example, your neighbour happens to be Turkish.

Finally, your restaurant opens, but nobody shows up. Why not? The explanation cannot be that people in the neighbourhood do not like Turkish food, since 60 per cent do. The explanation cannot be that your prices are too high or that your dishes taste bad, because potential customers do not know your prices or quality yet. The explanation cannot be lack of advertising, because you have big banners, a fancy website and advertisements in local papers. Then you hear that someone has been spreading rumours that your restaurant is filled with cockroaches. Who? Nobody else would have a motive, so you suspect the owner of the older restaurant across the street. This conclusion is supported by an *inference to the best explanation*. It is also an inductive argument, because its premises give some reason to believe your conclusion, but your suspicions could still be wrong.

Although discouraged, you regain hope when you remember the story of another Turkish restaurant that had a rough first month but then later became extremely popular as soon as people tried it. That other restaurant is a lot like yours, so you conclude that your restaurant will probably take off soon. This *argument from analogy* is inductive, because it is clearly not valid but does give some reason for hope.

Luckily, your restaurant turns into a huge success. Customers pile in. What attracts them to your restaurant? To find out, you lower your prices a little, but that has no effect on turnout. Then you check your records to see which dishes customers ordered more often, but nothing sticks out. Your curiosity is piqued, so you drop items off your menu one by one and observe changes in the clientele. There is a big drop in customers when you take kokoreç off the menu. Kokoreç consists of lamb or goat intestines wrapped around seasoned hearts, lungs and kidneys. You had no idea that local people like offal so much, but your experiment supports the conclusion that this dish is what causes people to come to your restaurant. This *causal reasoning* is inductive, because it is possible that something else is the cause, so the argument is not valid, but it still gives you some reason to believe its conclusion. Accordingly, you put kokoreç back on your menu.

All goes well until your restaurant is robbed. The only witness reports that the robber drove off in a Fiat. Only a small percentage (2 per cent) of the cars in Edinburgh are Fiats, so the witness's report is surprising, and you wonder whether to trust it. You and the police estimate that this witness in these lighting conditions will identify a Fiat correctly around 90 per cent of the time and will misidentify another kind of car as a Fiat around 10 per cent of the time. That sounds pretty good, but then (using Bayes' theorem) you calculate that the probability of this report being accurate is less than one in six.[4] It is five times more likely that the witness misidentified another car as a Fiat. This argument exemplifies *reasoning about probability*.

This story could go on, but it already includes six kinds of inductive arguments: statistical generalization, statistical application, inference to the best explanation, argument from analogy, causal reasoning and probability. Each of these forms of argument is common in many areas of everyday life. Each has its own standards and can be performed well or poorly. Each has special fallacies associated only with it. Instead of surveying them all, I will focus on a few of the most important kinds of inductive argument.[5]

How can dates and polls go wrong?

Profiling and stereotypes are anathema to many people. Police are supposed to choose whom to stop or arrest by observing what those people do instead of what they look like or where they are. In everyday life, many people aspire to Martin Luther King's vision: 'I have a dream that my four little children will one day live in a nation where they will not be judged by the colour of their skin but by the content of their character.'[6] We all hope to be treated as individuals rather than as members of groups.

Despite these hopes and dreams, we all use stereotypes about groups to predict how other individuals will act. Marketing experts use generalizations about groups to predict which customers will buy their products, as with our Turkish restaurant. Doctors use risk factors – which include group membership – to recommend medications and operations. Insurance agents charge individual clients on the basis of whether or not they belong to groups that cost insurers expensive payments. Universities decide which applicants to admit on the basis of their grades. We hope that these professionals will not judge customers, patients, clients or applicants by the colour of their skin, but they also do not base their decisions on the content of their character. They can't, because they don't know enough about their character.

In many contexts, it is hard to see how we could do without stereotypes. If I do not know someone at all, but I need to make a fast decision, then the only information I can use is what I can observe quickly. For example, if a stranger in a public bar talks casually with me for a few minutes and then offers to buy me a drink or dinner, then I need to decide whether to trust this stranger. What is he up to? As we saw, Sherlock Holmes might be able to induce a great deal about this stranger, but most of us have no choice but to rely on a few inaccurate generalizations based on our limited experience. We all do it, whether or not we accept the stranger's offer.

These cases depend on arguments up and down. First, they generalize *up* from premises about a sample of a group to a conclusion about the group as a whole. Second, they apply the resulting generalization back *down* to a conclusion about the individual. These two stages can be described as generalization and application.

GENERALIZATION

Each of these forms of argument introduces numerous complexities and complications. Even the most sophisticated reasoning of this sort can go badly wrong. Just recall the surprising mistakes made by political polls in the Brexit vote in the UK and also the 2016 Presidential election in the US. In those cases, even professional statisticians with tons of data were way off base. To avoid such errors and to fully understand statistical generalizations and applications, we all need to take several courses in statistics and probability, and then we need to gather big data of high quality. Who has the time? Luckily a simple example can illustrate a few common methods and mistakes without going into technical detail.

Imagine that you are seeking a male life partner who will play golf with you, and you are curious about online dating websites. You go onto one site, randomly pick ten potential dates, and ask each of them how often he played golf in the last six months. Only one of them reports having played golf at all in the last six months. You reason that only 10 per cent of your sample played golf in the last six months, so around 10 per cent of people who use online dating services play golf. This argument is a statistical generalization, because it runs from a premise about a sample (the ten you asked) to a conclusion about the whole group (people who use online dating sites).

The next day, someone else who uses the site contacts you. You decide not to reply, because you reason like this: 'This person uses an online dating website, and only 10 per cent of online dating website users play golf, so this person probably does not play golf – or, more precisely, there is only a 10 per cent chance that this person played golf in the last six months.' This argument is a statistical application, because it applies premises that include a generalization about the whole group to a conclusion about this particular user.

Both of these arguments are inductive, because they are

clearly not valid. It is possible that only 10 per cent of your sample plays golf, but many more people who use online dating services play golf. It is also possible that 10 per cent of people who use online dating services play golf, but it is much more likely that this individual plays golf. Because these possibilities are so obvious, this argument is probably not intended to be valid.

How strong are these inductive arguments? That depends on the probability of the conclusion given the premises. To assess that, we need to ask a series of questions to determine how each argument could go astray.

The first question to ask about the generalization is whether its premise is true. Did only one out of your sample of ten play golf in the last six months? Even if only one reported playing golf then, maybe more of them played golf, but they chose to ignore that question; or maybe they played golf but forgot about it; or maybe they denied playing golf because they thought you were asking your question in order to weed out dates who play golf too often. People on online dating sites are not always trustworthy. What a surprise!

The second question is whether your sample is big enough. It is better to ask ten than to ask only three, but it would be better yet to ask a hundred, although it would take a long time to gather such a large sample. A sample of ten thus gives your argument some strength, but not much. Whether it is strong enough depends on how much is at stake. If the sample is too small, then the argument commits a fallacy called *hasty generalization*.

The third question is whether your sample is biased. A sample is biased when the percentage of the sample with the feature you are seeking is significantly higher or lower than the percentage of the whole group with that feature. Notice that even a large sample (such as 100 or 1,000 online daters) can be biased. This bias could occur if most golfers use a different online dating website, which reduces the number of golfers who use the website that you are sampling. Then you should not use your sample to draw any conclusion about how many people who use online dating services in general play golf. Even if you are interested only in this particular website, your sample might be biased if your application mentioned that you play golf, and the website used this information to suggest possible contacts. Then the names that you received might include many more golfers than is representative of the website as a whole. Or the website might send you only names of local users, and you might live in an area with fewer (or more) golfers than other areas.

Another way to bias your sample is by asking leading or misleading questions. The percentage of affirmative answers would probably have been much higher if you had asked, 'Would you ever be willing to play golf?' and much lower if you had asked, 'Are you fanatical about golf?' To avoid this way of pushing your results in one direction or the other, you asked, 'How often did you play golf in the last six months?' This apparently neutral question still might have hidden biases. If you ask it in April, many golfers in snowy climates will not have played golf in six months, even though they will play as much as they can after the snow melts and their golf courses open. To avoid this problem, you should have asked about a full year. Or maybe they really do like to play golf, but they have nobody to play with, so they are also looking for a partner who plays golf. Then you should have asked whether they want to play golf. The results of generalizations are often affected by the questions used to gather a sample.

Overall, every inductive generalization from a sample needs to meet several standards. First, its premises must be true. (Duh! That is obvious, but people often forget it.) Second, its sample must be large enough. (Obvious again! But people rarely bother to ask how big the sample was.) Third, its sample must not be biased. (Bias is often less clear, because it is hidden in the sampling methods.) You will be fooled less often if you get in to the habit of asking whether all three standards are met whenever you encounter or give an inductive generalization.

APPLICATION

The next kind of induction applies generalizations back down to individuals. Our example was this argument: 'This person uses an online dating website, and only 10 per cent of online dating website users play golf, so this person probably does not play golf.' How strong is this argument?

As always, the first question that you need to ask is whether its premises are true. If not (and if you should know this), then this argument does not give you a strong reason to believe the conclusion. But let's assume that the premises are true.

You also need to ask whether the percentage is high (or low) enough. Your argument would provide a stronger reason for its conclusion if its second premise cited 1 per cent instead of 10 per cent and a weaker reason for its conclusion if its second premise cited 30 per cent instead of 10 per cent. And if its second premise were that 90 per cent of online daters play golf, then it could provide a strong reason for the opposite conclusion that this person probably *does* play golf. These numbers affect the strength of this kind of inductive argument.

Another kind of mistake is more subtle and quite common. What if the person who contacts you on the dating website contacted you because your profile mentioned golf? Add that 80 per cent of users who contact people because their profiles mention golf are themselves golfers. We can build this new information into a conflicting statistical application. This person contacted you because your profile mentioned golf, and 80 per cent of users who contact people because their profiles mention golf are themselves golfers, so this person probably does play golf – or, more precisely, there is an 80 per cent chance that this person plays golf.

Now we have statistical applications with opposite conclusions. The first said that this person probably does not play golf. The second says that this person probably does play golf. Which is more accurate? Which should we trust? The crucial difference to notice is that these arguments cite different classes, called *reference classes*. The first argument cites percentages within the class of online dating website users, whereas the second cites percentages within the class of those special online dating website users who contact people because their profiles mention golf. The latter class is smaller and a proper subset of the former class. In cases like this, assuming that the premises are true and equally justified, the argument with the narrower reference class usually provides a stronger reason, because its information is more specific to the case at hand.

Conflicting reference classes are often overlooked by people who apply generalizations to individual conclusions. This mistake combined with the fallacy of hasty generalization lies behind a great deal of stereotyping and prejudice. We all depend on generalizations and stereotypes in some cases, but mistakes about disadvantaged and vulnerable ethnic, racial and gender groups can be especially harmful. A bigot might run into one stupid, violent or dishonest member of an ethnic group. Every group has bad apples. The bigot then hastily generalizes to the conclusion that everyone in that ethnic group is similarly stupid, violent or dishonest. Then the bigot meets a new member of that ethnic group and applies the hasty generalization. The bigot concludes that this new individual is also stupid, violent or dishonest, without considering the fact that this new individual also has other features that indicate intelligence, pacifism and honesty. The bigot's small sample and failure to consider such narrow conflicting reference classes show how bad reasoning can play a role in originating and maintaining prejudice. Bad reasoning is not the whole story, of course, since emotion, history and self-interest also fuel bigotry, but we still might be able to reduce prejudice to some degree by avoiding simple mistakes in inductive arguments.

Why did that happen?

Our next form of inductive reasoning is inference to the best explanation. It might be the most common form of all. When a cake does not rise, the baker needs to figure out the best explanation of this catastrophe. When a committee member does not show up to a meeting, colleagues wonder why. When a car does not start in the morning, its owner needs to find the best explanation in order to figure out which part to fix. This kind of inductive argument is also what detectives (like Sherlock Holmes) use to catch criminals. Detectives infer a conclusion about who did it, because that conclusion provides the best explanation of their observations of the crime scene, the suspects and other evidence. Many crime dramas are, in effect, long inferences to the best explanation. Science also postulates theories as the best explanation of observed results in experiments, such as when Sir Isaac Newton postulates gravity to explain tides or palaeontologists hypothesize a meteor to explain the extinction of the dinosaurs. These arguments share a certain form:

(1) *Observation*: some surprising phenomenon needs to be explained.
(2) *Hypothesis*: a certain hypothesis explains the observations in (1).
(3) *Comparison*: the explanation in (2) is better than any alternative explanation of the observations in (1).
(4) *Conclusion*: the hypothesis in (2) is correct.

In our examples, the observations in (1) are the cake not rising, the colleague missing the meeting, the car not starting, the crime occurring, the tides rising and the dinosaurs disappearing. Each argument then needs a set of competing hypotheses to compare, plus some reasons to prefer one of those explanations.

Inferences to the best explanation are clearly not valid, since it is possible for the conclusion (4) to be false when the premises (1)–(3) are all true. That lack of validity is, however, a feature rather than a bug. Inferences to the best explanation are not intended to be valid, so it is unfair to criticize them for failing to be valid – just as it would be unfair to criticize a bicycle for failing to work in the ocean.

Inferences to the best explanation still need to meet other standards. They can go astray when any of their premises is false. Sometimes an inference to the best explanation is defective because the observation in premise (1) is not accurate. A detective might be misled when he tries to explain the blood on the car seat, when the stain is really beetroot juice. An inference to the best explanation can also go astray when the hypothesis in premise (2) does not really explain the observation. You might think that your car did not start because it was out of fuel, when actually the starter did not even begin to turn over, and lack of fuel cannot explain that observation, since the starter does turn over when it is out of fuel (but not when the electrical system fails). Perhaps the most common problem for inferences to the best explanation is when premise (3) is false either because a competing hypothesis is better than the arguer thinks or because the arguer overlooked an alternative hypothesis that provides an even better explanation. You might think that your colleague missed the meeting because she forgot, when really she was hit by a car on the way to the meeting. Such mistakes can lead to regret and apologies.

Overall, some inferences to the best explanation can provide strong reasons to believe their conclusions, as when a detective provides evidence beyond a reasonable doubt that a defendant is guilty. In contrast, other inferences to the best explanation fail miserably, such as when beetroot juice is mistaken for blood. In order to determine how strong an inference to the best explanation is, we need to look carefully at each premise and also at the conclusion.

HUSSEIN'S TUBES

Let's try this with a controversial example. Some of the most important inferences to the best explanation lie behind political decisions, such as the decision by the United States to start the Iraq War. In his testimony before the United Nations Security Council on 5 February 2003, US Secretary of State Colin Powell gave this argument:

> Saddam Hussein is determined to get his hands on a
> nuclear bomb. He is so determined that he has made
> repeated covert attempts to acquire high-specification
> aluminum tubes from eleven different countries . . . There
> is controversy about what these tubes are for. Most US
> experts think they are intended to serve as rotors in
> centrifuges to enrich uranium. Other experts, and the
> Iraqis themselves, argue that they are really to produce the
> rocket bodies for a conventional weapon, a multiple rocket
> launcher . . . First, it strikes me as quite odd that these
> tubes are manufactured to a tolerance that far exceeds US
> requirements for comparable rockets. Maybe Iraqis just
> manufacture their conventional weapon to a higher
> standard than we do, but I don't think so. Second, we
> actually have examined tubes from several different
> batches that were seized clandestinely before they reached
> Baghdad. What we notice in these different batches is a

progression to higher and higher levels of specification . . . Why would they continue refining the specifications, go to all that trouble for something that, if it was a rocket, would soon be blown into shrapnel when it went off? . . . [T]ese illicit procurement efforts show that Saddam Hussein is very much focused on putting in place the key missing piece from his nuclear weapons program, the ability to produce fissile material.[7]

Of course, I do not endorse this argument. There are many reasons to doubt its premises and conclusion, especially given what we learned later. My goal is only to understand it.

The most natural way to understand Powell's argument is as an inference to the best explanation. He mentions a surprising phenomenon that needs to be explained and compares three potential explanations of that phenomenon, so his argument fits cleanly into the form above:

(1*) *Observation*: Saddam Hussein made repeated covert attempts to acquire high-specification aluminum tubes that were increasingly refined.

(2*) *Hypothesis*: Hussein's desire to produce fissile material and use it to make a nuclear bomb could explain why he made the attempts described in (1*).

(3*) *Comparison*: the explanation in (2*) is better than any alternative explanation of the observations in (1*), including Hussein's reported desire to produce conventional rocket bodies and higher standards in Iraqi manufacturing.

(4*) *Conclusion*: Hussein desires to produce fissile material for a nuclear bomb.

Powell adds more to back up his premises, but let's start with the central argument (1*)–(4*). Reconstructing the argument in this form should reveal or clarify how its premises work together to provide some reason to believe its conclusion. But how strong is that reason? To assess the strength of the argument, we need to go through the premises and conclusion carefully.

Premise (1*) raises several questions. How high were the specifications of the tubes that Hussein tried to obtain? How do we know that he insisted on such high specifications? How many attempts did he make? How long ago? Were they covert in the sense of being hidden from everyone or only from the US? Why did he hide them? Although such questions are important, Powell could probably answer them, and he does cite evidence of Hussein's attempts in other parts of his testimony, so it makes sense here to focus attention on his other premises.

Premise (2*) adds that the phenomenon in (1*) can be explained by Hussein's desire to produce fissile material for a nuclear bomb. This makes sense. People who desire to make fissile material will want to acquire what is necessary to make it, and high-specification aluminum tubes were needed to produce fissile material. Indeed, the high specifications were needed only for fissile material of the kind used in nuclear bombs, and there would be little use for this kind of fissile material except in making nuclear bombs. At least that is what Powell assumes.

The most serious problems arise in premise (3*). This premise compares Powell's preferred explanation in (2*) with two competitors: a desire to produce conventional rocket bodies and higher Iraqi standards in manufacturing rockets. Powell focuses on rocket bodies, because that explanation was offered by Hussein himself. Still, Powell's argument would fail if any other explanation was as strong as Powell's preferred explanation in (2*), so we need to consider both alternatives.

Powell criticizes the alternative explanation in terms of conventional rockets by asking rhetorical questions: 'Why would they continue refining the specifications, go to all that trouble for something that, if it was a rocket, would soon be blown into shrapnel when it went off?' His point here is that the explanation in terms of conventional rockets fails to explain the continual refinements, because rockets do not require these refinements, whereas his preferred explanation in terms of nuclear bombs succeeds in explaining these additional observations. Its ability to explain more observations is what is supposed to make his explanation better.

This increased explanatory power is a common ground for preferring one explanation to another. Suppose that the hypothesis that Gregor killed Maxim explains why the bootprints outside the murder scene are size 14, because Gregor wears size 14 boots, but this hypothesis cannot explain why those bootprints have their distinctive tread pattern, because Gregor does not own any boots with that tread pattern. Then that explanation is not as good as the hypothesis that Ivan killed Maxim, if Ivan wears size 14 and also owns boots with that distinctive tread pattern. We prefer hypotheses that explain more. Powell is simply applying this general principle to the case of aluminium tubes.

This argument is still subject to many objections. Critics could deny or doubt that Iraq did continue refining the specifications, in which case there would be no need to explain this. Or they could reply that these continual refinements were needed for conventional rockets, so the alternative hypothesis does explain the observations. To avoid these objections, Powell needs background arguments that are not included in the quoted passage. Still, even without delving deeper, our reconstruction has pinpointed at least two issues for further exploration.

The other alternative that Powell mentions is that 'Iraqis just manufacture their conventional weapons to a higher standard than we do.' Here Powell seems to have his tongue in his cheek. That is why he thinks all he needs to say in response is simply, 'I don't think so.' This sarcastic assurance seems to build on the assumption that US manufacturing is at least as precise as Iraqi manufacturing. That assumption might be obvious to this audience, but it is striking that Powell does not explicitly give any reason to favour his own explanation above this alternative.

It need not always be a problem to ignore or dismiss an alternative explanation without argument. Some alternative explanations are so clearly inadequate that they do not deserve any effort at refutation. Every inference to the best explanation would need to be irritatingly long in order to deal with every foolish alternative. Nonetheless, this failure to argue against an alternative does reduce the potential audience for the argument. It cannot reach anyone with any inclination to accept this alternative explanation.

The most serious weakness in Powell's argument lies not in the alternatives he does mention, but in the alternatives he does *not* mention. This problem pervades inferences to the best explanation. Just recall any murder mystery in which a new suspect appears after the detectives thought that they had already solved the case. The same kind of possibility can undermine Powell's argument, but here the suspects are hypotheses. In order to refute his argument, all that Powell's opponents need to produce is one other viable hypothesis that explains the relevant data at least as well as Powell's.

Notice that opponents do not have to produce a better alternative. If all they *want* to show is that he has not justi-fied his conclusion, then all they *need* to show is that there is one alternative at least as good as his. If two alternative explanations tie for top place, then Powell's argument cannot determine which of these top two is correct. In that case, Powell's opponents win, because Powell is the one who is trying to argue for one of them over the other.

Still, it might be hard to come up with even one decent alternative. Maybe Hussein was controlled by aliens who eat fissile material, but he did not want any for himself. You cannot falsify that alternative hypothesis if there is no way to detect the presence of such aliens. Nonetheless, these aliens would violate well-established laws of physics, so we have plenty of reasons to dismiss this hypothesis as silly. A little more realistically, maybe Hussein had OCD (obsessive-compulsive disorder), and that is why he continually demanded more refined tubes. However, he did not show symptoms of OCD in other areas of his life, so there is no independent evi-dence that he had this mental disorder (though maybe he had others, such as narcissism). Hypotheses like these are clearly not even decent explanations.

What we really need for a realistic explanation to be as good as Powell's is some common and plausible motive that would make Hussein seek more and more refined aluminium tubes. Well, maybe he wanted to use these tubes in some innocent kind of manufacturing. Maybe, but that hypothesis lacks explanatory power – it cannot explain much – until we make it more specific. What kind of products are such refined tubes needed to manufacture? The hypothesis that Hussein was planning to use the tubes to manufacture some other product also cannot explain why Hussein mentioned only conventional rockets in his defence. And Powell has already rejected the rocket hypothesis.

Thus it is at least not easy to come up with any explanation that is as good as Powell's. Of course, this difficulty might be due to my (and your?) lack of knowledge about rockets, fissile material and Iraqi manufacturing. Even if we cannot come up with any viable alternative, there still might be some explanation that is as good as Powell's. Nonetheless, in the absence of any such alternative, Powell's argument does give us some reason to believe his conclusion.

Other problems arise, however, when we look closely at that conclusion. The conclusion of an inference to the best explanation is supposed to be the same as the hypothesis that explains the observations. However, people who use this form of argument often make subtle changes in their conclusions. That happens here. First, Hussein's attempts to acquire the tubes occurred in the past. What explains these attempts is a desire at the past time when those attempts were made. However, the conclusion is about the present: Hussein desires – not desired – to produce fissile material for a nuclear bomb. Powell exchanged 's' for 'd'! Moreover, the present tense is essential. Powell wants to justify invading Iraq soon after his testimony. His argument would not work if Hussein used to desire fissile material in the past, but no longer has that desire at present. So Powell at least owes us some reason to believe that Hussein has not changed.

Similarly, what if Hussein still desires fissile material for a nuclear bomb, but he has little or no chance of getting any of what he desires? The Rolling Stones are right again: you can't always get what you want. Then the conclusion that Hussein wants fissile material for nuclear bombs would hardly be enough to justify invading Iraq. A lot of other world leaders want nuclear bombs, but the US is not justified in invading all of them. An invasion could be justified only if it would avoid some harm or danger, but a mere desire for nuclear bombs without any chance of fulfilling that desire would not be harmful or dangerous – or at least not harmful or dangerous enough to justify invasion. Thus Powell also owes us some reason to believe that Hussein has a significant chance of getting nuclear bombs.

These gaps show that Powell's argument is at best incomplete. As before, my job here is not to determine whether he was correct, much less whether the United States was justified in invading Iraq. I doubt it, partly because of what we have learned in intervening years, but that does not matter in this context. My goal is only to understand Powell and his argument better. Admitting these gaps in his argument is completely compatible with admitting that his argument still achieves something: it gives us some reason to believe the conclusion that Hussein desired to produce fissile material

PART THREE

How Not to Argue

How to Avoid Fallacies

There's good news and bad news. Good arguments are valuable, but bad arguments can be devastating, as we saw in Colin Powell's testimony to the United Nations. In less extreme cases, bad arguments can mislead us into wasting money on superfluous insurance or unreliable used cars, believing fairy tales and delusions, and adopting destructive government programmes as well as failing to adopt constructive government programmes. These dangers make it crucial to recognize and avoid bad arguments.

Bad arguments can obviously be intentional or unintentional. Sometimes speakers present arguments that they *see* as good, even though their arguments are really bad. These are mistakes. In other cases, speakers know that their arguments are bad, but they use them anyway to fool others. These are tricks. The argument can be equally bad in either case. The only difference lies in the arguer's awareness and intention. It is important to detect fallacies in both cases.

The idiosyncrasies and variety of bad arguments preclude any complete survey, but many bad arguments do fall into general patterns called *fallacies*. We already saw several common fallacies, including affirming the consequent and denying the antecedent in deductive arguments, plus hasty generalization and overlooking conflicting reference classes in inductive arguments. Of course, false premises can make any argument bad regardless of its form.

This chapter will introduce several more kinds of fallacies that often lead people astray. I will focus on three general groups of fallacies that are especially common.

What do you mean?

Our definition of arguments revealed not only the purpose and form of arguments but also their material: arguments are made of language. Both premises and conclusions are propositions expressed by declarative sentences in some language. It should come as no surprise, then, that arguments fall apart when language breaks down, just as bridges fall apart when there are cracks in the material out of which they are made.

Language can crack in many ways, but here the two most common and important defects are vagueness and ambiguity. *Vagueness* occurs when words or sentences are not precise enough for the context. In a scavenger hunt, instructions to find something tall are too vague if players do not know whether they can win by producing a person somewhat above average height. In contrast, *ambiguity* occurs when a word has two distinct meanings, and it is not clear which meaning the speaker intends. If I promise to meet you next to the bank, then I had better tell you whether I mean the commercial bank or the river bank. A single word can sometimes be both vague and ambiguous, such as when it matters where exactly the river bank ends.

DOUBLE ENTENDRE

Ambiguity is rampant in newspaper headlines. One of my favourite examples is 'Mrs Gandhi Stoned in Rally in India'.[1] Yes, a newspaper actually printed that headline. It can mean either that the crowd threw stones at Mrs Gandhi or that she took drugs that intoxicated her. You had to read the article to find out. Another favourite is 'Police Kill Man With Axe'. Here the issue is not that a single word like 'stoned' changes meaning, but instead that the man might be 'with axe' or the police might be 'with axe'. When grammar or syntax creates ambiguity like this, it is called *amphiboly*. Either kind of ambiguity can produce amusement not only in headlines but also in jokes, such as 'I wondered why the Frisbee was getting bigger, and then it hit me.'[2]

Such ambiguity can ruin arguments. Imagine someone arguing, 'My neighbour had a friend for dinner. Anyone who has a friend for dinner is a cannibal. Cannibals should be punished. Therefore, my neighbour should be punished.' This argument is fallacious, but why? Its first premise seems to mean that my neighbour invited a friend over to his house to eat dinner. In contrast, its second premise refers to people who eat friends for dinner. These premises use different meanings of the phrase 'had a friend for dinner'. And if the whole argument sticks with the same meaning in both premises, then one of the premises comes out clearly false. The first premise is not true (I hope) if it means that my neighbour ate a friend for dinner. The second premise is not true if it refers to people who have friends over to their houses for dinner. Thus the argument fails on either interpretation. This fallacy is called *equivocation*.

A more serious example is the widespread argument that homosexuality is unnatural, so it must be immoral. This argument clearly depends on the suppressed premise that what is unnatural is immoral. Adding that extra premise, the argument looks like this: (1) Homosexuality is unnatural. (2) Everything unnatural is immoral. Therefore, (3) homosexuality is immoral.

The force of this argument depends on the word 'unnatural'. What does 'unnatural' mean here? It might mean that homosexuals violate laws of nature, but that cannot be correct. Homosexuality is not a miracle, so premise (1) must be false in this sense of 'unnatural'. Instead, premise (1) might mean that homosexuality is abnormal or an exception to generalities in nature. This premise is true, simply because homosexuality is statistically uncommon. But now, is premise (2) true? What is immoral about being statistically uncommon? It is also uncommon to play the sitar or to remain celibate, but sitar-playing and celibacy are not immoral. On a third interpretation, premise (1) might mean that homosexuality is artificial rather than a product of nature alone, as in food with 'all natural' ingredients. But again, what is wrong with that? Some artificial ingredients taste good and are good for you. So premise (2) again comes out false on this interpretation.

These critics of homosexuality might mean something more sophisticated, such as contrary to evolved purposes. This interpretation is more charitable and plausible. Their idea might be that it is dangerous to go against evolution, such as when someone tries to hammer a nail with his head, since our heads did not evolve to pound nails. This principle, plus the added premises that the evolved purpose of sex organs is to produce children and that homosexuals use their sex organs for purposes other than to produce children, might seem to support the conclusion that homosexuality is dangerous or immoral.

How can homosexuals and their allies respond to this argument? First, they can deny that the only evolutionary purpose of sex organs is to produce children. We also evolved in such a way that sex can bring pleasure and express love in heterosexuals as well as homosexuals. There is nothing unnatural about those other purposes. Sex can serve many evolutionary purposes. Second, defenders of homosexuality can deny that it is always dangerous or immoral to use bodily organs apart from their evolved purposes. Our ears did not evolve to hold jewellery, but that does not make it immoral to wear earrings. By the same token, the claim that homosexuals do not use their sex organs for their evolved purposes also would not show anything immoral about homosexuality.

Finally, the argument might use 'unnatural' to mean something like 'contrary to God's plan, intention, or design for nature'. The main problem with this move is to show why defenders of homosexuality should accept premise (1), which now claims that homosexuality is contrary to God's plan or design. This premise assumes that God exists, that God has a relevant plan and that homosexuality violates that plan. Many critics of homosexuality accept those assumptions, but their opponents do not. Thus it is not clear how this argument is supposed to have any force against anyone who did not already agree with its conclusion.

Overall, then, this argument that homosexuality is immoral because it is unnatural suffers from a central ambiguity. It commits the fallacy of equivocation. This criticism does not end the discussion. Defenders of the argument can still try to respond by delivering a different meaning of 'unnatural' that makes its premises true and justified. Alternatively, opponents of homosexuality could shift to a different argument. But they need to do something. The burden is on them. They cannot rely on this simple argument in its present form if it equivocates.

This example illustrates a pattern of questions that we should ask every time we suspect a fallacy of equivocation. First, ask which word seems to change meaning. Then ask which different meanings that word could have. Then specify one of those meanings at each point where that word occurs in the argument. Then ask whether the premises come out true and provide enough reason for the conclusion under that interpretation. If one of these interpretations yields a strong argument, that one meaning is enough for the argument to work. But if none of these interpretations yields a strong argument, then the argument commits the fallacy of equivocation, unless you simply failed to find the meaning that saves the argument.

SLIP SLIDING AWAY

The second way for language to lack clarity is vagueness. Vagueness is explored in a massive literature in philosophy,[3] which discusses such pressing issues as how many grains it takes to make a heap of sand. Vagueness also raises practical issues every day.

My friends often show up late. Don't yours? Suppose Maria agreed to meet you around noon for lunch, and she arrives at one second after noon. That is still around noon, isn't it? What if she arrives two seconds after noon? That's still around noon, right? Three seconds? Four seconds? You would not accuse her of being late if she arrived thirty seconds after noon, would you? Moreover, one more second cannot make a difference to whether or not she is late. It would be implausible to claim that fifty-nine seconds after noon is not late, but sixty seconds after noon *is* late. Now we have a paradox: Maria is not late if she arrives one second after noon. One second more cannot make her late if she was not late already. These premises together imply that she cannot ever be late even if she arrives a full hour after noon, since an hour is just a series of one second after another. The problem is that this conclusion is clearly false, because she is definitely late if she arrives an hour after noon.

This paradox arises partly because we started with the vague term 'around noon'. There would be no (or less) paradox if Maria agreed to meet you before noon. But that is the point. Vagueness leads to paradox, and we cannot avoid using vague terms in our everyday speech, so how can we avoid paradox? We can't.

Does this paradox matter? It does if we want to understand vagueness theoretically. It also matters practically if Maria is so late that we need to decide whether to complain or leave or order lunch without her. At what time do such actions become justified? I recall sitting for many minutes wondering about this issue.

No matter how long we wait, we definitely should not reach some conclusions. Several philosophers argue in effect that nobody is ever really late, because there is no precise time at which someone becomes late (at least when they promise to arrive around noon). Some also conclude that there is no real difference between being on time and being late. This kind of reasoning is a *conceptual* slippery-slope argument. It makes punctuality unavoidable, because you cannot ever really be late.

A different kind of slippery slope focuses not on concepts but instead on causal effects. A *causal* slippery-slope argument claims that an otherwise innocuous action will probably lead you down a slippery slope that ends in disaster, so you should not do that first action. If Maria arrives one minute late, and nobody complains, then her minor tardiness might make her more likely to arrive two minutes late the next time, and then three minutes late, and then four minutes late, and so on. Slippery slopes like this lead to bad habits.

How do we deal with these problems? We draw lines. If Maria starts to show up too late, then we might tell Maria, 'If you are not there by 12:15, then I will leave.' We also have to carry out this threat, but there's nothing wrong with that, if Maria was warned. It might seem problematic to be so arbitrary. However, although it is arbitrary to pick 12.15 instead of 12:14 or 12:16, we still do have reasons to draw some line (how else are we going to get Maria to stop showing up later and later?), and we also have reasons to locate our line within a certain area (after 12:01 and before 1:00). Our reasons for drawing a line between limits solve the practical problem of slippery-slope arguments, even if they leave many philosophical issues up in the air.

Tardy friends are annoying, but other slippery-slope arguments raise much more serious issues, such as torture. Torture is immoral in almost all cases, but the guarding term 'almost' is crucial. There is no justification for useless torture, as at Abu Ghraib, but some ethicists defend torture when it is likely to avoid extreme harm, as in ticking time-bomb cases. Imagine that the police capture an admitted terrorist who has planted a time bomb that will kill many people soon if not defused. The police can stop the slaughter if and only if the terrorist tells them where the bomb is, but he refuses to talk. There is some chance that he will reveal the bomb's location if they inflict enough pain on him, such as by waterboarding.

Such cases are controversial, but the point here is just that common arguments on both sides depend on vagueness and slippery slopes. One continuum is the number of people who would be harmed if the bomb went off. There is no precise number needed to justify torture. Another continuum is probability. Torture usually produces false information, but still has some chance of success. It is impossible to say precisely how high the probability of gaining accurate information needs to be in order to justify torture to save a certain number of lives. A third continuum is the amount of suffering caused by torture. Waterboarding for a minute is one thing, but it can go on for hours. And what about beating, burning and electrocuting? Are they also allowed? How much? How long? Again, it is impossible to say precisely how much pain is permitted for a specific increase in the chances of saving a specific number of lives.

These continuums enable conceptual slippery-slope arguments. Here's one: Police would not be justified in inflicting extreme pain only in order to reduce the chances of a terrorist stink bomb by 0.00001 per cent. A tiny increase in the amount of harm prevented or in the probability of success or a tiny decrease in the amount of pain inflicted cannot change unjustified torture into justified torture. The same goes for the next tiny increment and so on. Therefore, no torture – indeed, no infliction of any pain during interrogation – is ever justified.

This argument is reversible. Police would be justified in making a suspect sit in an uncomfortable chair for a minute in order to reduce the chances by 10 per cent of a nuclear explosion that will kill millions. A tiny decrease in the number of people saved or in the probability of success or a tiny increase in the amount of pain cannot change justified interrogation into unjustified torture. The same goes for the next tiny increment and so on down the slippery slope. Therefore, no torture is ever *un*justified.

When an argument runs equally smoothly in either direction, it fails in both directions, because it cannot give any reason why one conclusion is better than its opposite. The general lesson is that we all need to test our own arguments by asking whether opponents can give similar arguments on the other side. If so, that symmetry is a strong indication that our own argument is inadequate as it stands.

That lesson still does not tell us how to stop sliding down the slippery slope. One potential solution is definition. The US government at one point declared that interrogation is not torture unless it causes pain equivalent to organ failure.[4] That definition was supposed to allow interrogators to waterboard suspects for a long time without engaging in torture. However, opponents could simply define torture more broadly. They might say, for example, that police torture whenever they intentionally cause any physical pain. Then even a few seconds of waterboarding counts as torture, but so does requiring suspects to stand (or sit in an uncomfortable chair) for an hour if that is intended to make them more compliant. Thus, as before, opponents can make the same move in opposite directions.

Nonetheless, definitions do provide some glimmer of hope. It is not enough for such definitions to capture common usage, as in a dictionary. Common usage is too vague to resolve this issue. Instead, definitions of torture aim at a practical or moral goal. They try to (and should) group together all cases that are similar in moral respects. As a result, opponents can discuss which definition achieves this goal. That debate will be complex and controversial, but at least we know what needs to be done in order to make progress on this issue: we need to determine which definition leads to the most defensible laws and policies.

What about the causal slippery slope? Here the two sides are not as symmetrical. If we start waterboarding a little bit, this first step onto the slippery slope seems likely to break down psychological, institutional and legal barriers to torture, which will lead to waterboarding for longer periods of time in more situations with less harm to avoid and less chance of success. That causal slippery slope could eventually lead to widespread unjustified torture. In the other direction, if we reduce extreme torture a little bit, it seems much less likely that this minor mercy will make police give up interrogation entirely. The strong motives for interrogation will probably stop that causal slippery slope from leading to disaster. Thus, the causal slippery-slope argument against torture cannot be dismissed as symmetrical in the same way as the conceptual slippery-slope argument for the same conclusion.

As always, I am not endorsing this argument or its conclusion. Indeed, classifying it as a causal slippery slope instead of a conceptual slippery slope reveals places where opponents can object. This argument depends on a controversial prediction: a little bit of waterboarding will eventually cause a lot of waterboarding. That premise might be accurate, but it is not obvious, especially because institutions can adopt rules that limit the degree and amount of torture that is allowed. If we want to avoid extreme torture, two options might work. One is to forbid all torture. Another is to enforce rules that limit torture. Of course, opponents of all torture will deny that such limits can be enforced effectively, but they need to argue for that claim. In reply, defenders of limited torture need to show how institutions really could restrict torture effectively. It is not clear how to establish either of these conflicting premises, but our analysis of these arguments as causal slippery slopes has made progress by locating and clarifying the crucial issue.

Whether or not you accept the argument against torture, it reveals what we need to do in order to assess any slippery-slope argument. First determine whether the slippery slope is conceptual or causal. If it is conceptual, ask whether the slope is equally slippery in the opposite direction and whether the problem can be solved by a definition that is justified by its practical or theoretical benefits. If the slippery slope is causal, ask whether setting foot on the slope really will lead to disaster. Asking and answering these questions can help us determine which slippery slopes we really do need to avoid.

Can I trust you?

Our second group of fallacies raises questions about when premises are relevant to the conclusion. It is surprising how often arguments jump from premises about one topic to a conclusion about a different topic.

Blatant examples occur when people fail to answer the question that was asked. This scam saturates political debates and undermines understanding. We all need to learn to spot it and stop it. We need to notice when people fail to answer questions and then call them out publicly.

Here we will focus on more subtle instances of irrelevance. Specifically, many arguments present premises about a person as reasons for a conclusion about some proposition or belief. These arguments can be positive or negative. One might argue, 'He's a bad person, so what he says is false.' Alternatively, one might argue, 'He's a good person, so what he says is true.' The former is described as an *ad hominem* argument, whereas the latter is an *appeal to authority*. The difference lies in whether the argument invites me to distrust or to trust the person.

ATTACKING PEOPLE

Here is a classic example of the negative pattern:

> It's an interesting question: Why do so many political protesters tend to be, to put it mildly, physically ugly? . . . [I]t is simply a visual fact that the students and non-students marching in these picket lines with hand-lettered

placards are mostly quite unattractive human beings . . .
They are either too fat or too thin, they tend to be strangely
proportioned . . . But if nature failed to give most of these
people much to work with, they themselves have not
improved matters much. Ill-fitting blue jeans seem to be
the uniform. Sloppy shirts. Hair looks unkempt, unwashed.
They wear a variety of stupid-looking shoes. Yuck . . .[5]

This writer is clearly trying to get readers to distrust and dismiss the protesters because of their appearance.

It is hard to imagine that anyone would be misled by such a blatant fallacy, but sometimes it does work by associating the target with negative feelings such as disgust, contempt or fear. These negative emotions can produce distrust, even when the features that trigger the negative emotions are irrelevant to the topic at hand. This trick has been used to exclude the views of dissident groups throughout history. It might also lie behind laws (throughout much of the United States) that deprive ex-felons of a right to vote, even on issues which they know and care a lot about, such as criminal policy. And it infects criminal trials when juries distrust a rape victim's allegations because she had previously had voluntary sex more than they think proper.

Ad hominem arguments vary in flavour. The most flagrant fallacy occurs when someone argues, 'She has a bad feature, so what she says must be false.' A less blatant form occurs when reliability is doubted, as in 'She has a bad feature, so you cannot trust what she says.' The crucial difference between these two variations is that the former concludes that a claim is false, whereas the latter leaves us not knowing what to believe. A third version denies someone's right to speak at all, 'She has a bad feature, so she has no right to speak on this topic.' This conclusion again does not tell us what to believe, because it leaves open the question of whether her views would be true and reliable if she did speak. Often, as in the quotation above, it is not clear which of these points is being made, even though the point lies somewhere in this general area.

Each kind of ad hominem fallacy is able to mislead partly because other arguments of the same kind do provide reasons for their conclusions. Spectators do not have the right to speak during parliamentary debates, no matter how reliable they would be if they did speak. You really should not trust someone who failed physics but takes a strong stand on a controversy in physics. And sometimes the features of people even give reasons to believe that what they say is false, such as when the owner of a cheap-clothing shop tells you that his products are made of the finest silk.

Despite this possibility, ad hominem arguments are fallacious often enough that they should be inspected with great suspicion. You should always take great care before reaching a conclusion about a belief from negative premises about the believer.

Unfortunately, people are rarely this careful. As we saw in Part One, conservatives often reject their opponents' views by calling their opponents liberal, just as liberals often dismiss their opponents' views by calling their opponents conservative. Such classifications commit ad hominem fallacies insofar as they use premises about the person being liberal or conservative to reach conclusions about particular claims by those people. Liberals are right sometimes, and so are conservatives, so it is very dubious to argue that any belief is true or false just because the believer is liberal or conservative.

The mistake is different when someone calls their opponents stupid or crazy. These are attributes of the person, so this argument is still an ad hominem. Nonetheless, it is legitimate to distrust the views of people who really are stupid or crazy, at least when their views are idiosyncratic. The main problem here is that the premises are usually false, because the person being attacked is not really stupid or crazy.

A general tendency to be fooled by these fallacies feeds the political polarization that impedes cooperation and social progress. When we dismiss opponents on the basis of what they are, we cut ourselves off from any hope of understanding them or learning from them. That is one reason why we need to be careful to avoid this kind of fallacy.

In general, whenever you encounter any ad hominem argument that moves from premises about a person's negative features to a conclusion about that person's claim, you should critically evaluate whether the premises are true and also whether the negative feature really is relevant to the truth of the claim, to the reliability of the person, or to the right of this person to speak on this issue. Asking these questions will help you reduce both personal errors and social polarization.

QUESTIONING AUTHORITY

The positive pattern of arguing from people to positions is at least as common as the negative pattern. The tendency to trust people whom we like or admire has been described as the halo effect (after angels with halos), and the tendency to distrust people who we dislike has been called a horn effect (after devils with horns). We are subject to both effects: halos and horns. We trust our allies as much as we distrust our opponents. Indeed, we often trust our allies too much.

When people trust an authority, they argue from premises about that authority to a conclusion about what that authority said. I might argue, 'My friend told me that our neighbour is having an affair, so our neighbour is having an affair.' This argument is only as strong as my friend is reliable on issues like this. Similarly, I might argue, 'This website or news channel told me that our President is having an affair, so our President is having an affair.' This argument is only as strong as this website or news channel is reliable on issues like this. If a friend or news channel is not reliable on issues like this, then sources like these do not deserve our trust on this issue. But if they are reliable, then they do deserve at least some trust, even if they disagree with us.

How can we tell whether a source of information is reliable on a particular issue? There is no foolproof test, but a good start is to ask a simple series of questions.

The first question that we always need to ask is simple: 'Did the arguer cite the authority correctly?' The news article that we reconstructed in Chapter 8 quoted Robert Jauncey and paraphrased an Asian Development Bank (ADB) report. We should have asked, 'Did Jauncey really say these precise words? Did the ADB really report what the article claims?' It is surprising how often people misquote authorities either intentionally or by mistake. Even when authorities are quoted accurately, their words are sometimes pulled out of context in ways that distort the meaning. Jauncey was quoted as saying, 'There has been a rapid rise of urban villages in recent years due to increased poverty and the negative impacts of climate change.' Now imagine that his next sentence was, 'Fortunately, these trends are slowing and even reversing, so we do not need to worry about urban villages in coming years.' If he had said this – he didn't, but if he had – then the quotation in the article would have been extremely misleading, even though he did say exactly what it reported that he said. Thus, whenever you encounter an appeal to authority, you should ask not only whether the appeal accurately reported the authority's words but also whether the appeal correctly represented the authority's meaning.

The second question to ask about appeals to authority is more complex: 'Can the cited authority be trusted to tell the truth?' Whereas the first question was about words and meanings, this second question is about motives. If the authority had some incentive to lie, or if the authority has a tendency to report its findings loosely or in misleading ways, then it cannot be trusted even when it is quoted correctly. For example, if Jauncey were trying to raise money for a charity that employs him, so that he would benefit personally if he could convince you to donate money to help solve problems of urban villages, then you would have reason to wonder whether he was exaggerating the problem for his own purposes. His self-interest then gives grounds for mistrust, since it could lead him to report a falsehood even when he knows the truth.

What should we do if an authority cannot be trusted because of self-interest or whatever? One approach is to check independent authorities. If different authorities do not depend on each other and have no motivation to promote the same view, but they still agree, then the best explanation of why they agree is usually that their belief is accurate – so we have reason to trust them. To justify trust, seek confirmation.

The third question is even trickier: 'Is the cited authority in fact an authority in the appropriate area?' It takes a lot of work to become an authority in even one area, so few people are able to achieve authority in a wide range of areas. People who know a lot about history usually do not know as much about mathematics, and vice versa. Real masters of all trades are extremely rare. Nonetheless, even when their expertise is limited to a specific topic, authorities often think that they know more about other topics than they actually do. Success in one area breeds overconfidence in others.

The most obvious cases occur when athletes endorse cars or other commercial products that have nothing to do with the sports in and on which they are experts. Sports heroes as well as actors, business leaders and military heroes also often endorse political candidates, even when there is little or no basis for assuming that these experts in their own fields know more than anyone else about political candidates or policies.

A similar problem arises in law. Psychiatrists and clinical psychologists are trained in diagnosis and treatment of mental illnesses, but lawyers sometimes ask them to predict the likelihood of future crimes by defendants. Are they authorities in this area? No, according to their own professional organization: 'It does appear from reading the research that the validity of psychological predictions of dangerous behaviour, at least in the sentencing and release situation we are considering, is extremely poor, so poor that one could oppose their use on the strictly empirical grounds that psychologists are not professionally competent to make such judgments.'[6] In short, authorities on psychiatric diagnosis and treatment are not authorities on the prediction of criminal behaviour. As a result, to appeal to their authority as a basis for legal decisions is fallacious. This fallacy can be uncovered and avoided by asking whether the cited authorities are authorities in the right area.

Fourth, we should ask, 'Is there agreement among appropriate experts on this issue?' Of course, there cannot be agreement among appropriate experts if there are no appropriate experts. Some issues cannot be settled by expert opinion. No group of experts now can settle whether there is life on Mars. They need more evidence than we have at present. No group of experts could ever settle which kind of fish tastes best. That is not the right kind of issue to settle conclusively. We can identify such gaps in expertise by asking whether this is the kind of question that can now be settled by expert consensus.

If so, we can next ask whether experts have reached agreement. Of course, unanimity is not required. There will always be a few dissenters, but the evidence can still be strong when almost all experts agree. Doctors have reached a consensus that smoking tobacco causes cancer. Of course, the experts have evidence for this claim, but few non-experts know any or many details of the studies that convinced the experts that smoking tobacco causes cancer. That is why we need to rely on expert authorities. When non-experts argue, 'Doctors agree that smoking causes cancer, so that's good enough for me to believe that it does', it would not make much sense to insist that they tell us how doctors reached that consensus. It is enough for non-experts to know that experts did reach a consensus.

In some cases, the appropriate kind of expert is simply a witness. The experts on whether a government official communicated with a foreign spy include witnesses who saw them meet or heard them talk. To get agreement between experts, then, is simply to have one witness confirm what the other said. As long as their shared story is not denied by other reliable sources, such confirmation can reduce the chance of error and justify belief. That is why most good news reporters wait to deliver stories only after they are confirmed by multiple independent sources.

A fifth question is about the motives of the person who appeals to an authority: 'Why is an appeal to authority being made at all?' When a claim is obvious, we can simply assert it and maybe also call it obvious. Then we do not need to add an appeal to any authority. It would be pointless to argue, 'Most mathematicians agree that 2 + 2 = 4, so it must be true.' Thus when someone does appeal to an authority, they usually make that appeal because they know that their claim is not obvious, at least to non-experts. Their appeal signals that they know their audience could reasonably raise questions, so they cite the authority in order to head off those questions. The best response, then, is to ask the very questions that they are hoping to avoid.

To see how these five questions work together, let's apply the series to science. Many people assume that science does not depend on any authority. In their view, religion and law depend on authorities, but science works purely by observation and experimentation. That is incorrect. Almost every scientific paper cites many authorities who have previously settled other issues so that this paper can build on those predecessors to address a new issue. Sir Isaac Newton, one of the greatest scientists of all time, said that he stood on the shoulders of giants, and he meant previous authorities.

What justifies scientists in trusting other scientists as authorities? After all, scientists are human, so they are fallible like the rest of us. The difference is that individual scientists work within larger groups and institutions that are structured to foster reliability. One virtue of science that is conducive to reliability is the insistence on replication by independent scientists or laboratories. Independent attempts at replication are unlikely to succeed when results are distorted by personal motives and mistakes. Another feature of science that breeds reliability is competition. When one scientist reports a new finding, other scientists have strong incentives to refute it. With so many smart people trying so hard to find mistakes, only the best theories survive. We have reason to trust any view that survives such a process.[7] Of course, many scientific theories have been overturned, and most scientific theories today will probably be overturned in the future. Nonetheless, we can still have reason to trust the best theories and data that we have now.

One important recent example is the Intergovernmental Panel on Climate Change (IPCC), which includes hundreds of top climate scientists from around the world.[8] This large and diverse group has worked long and hard to reach consensus about many, though far from all, aspects of climate change. Suppose that someone appeals to the IPCC as an authority to argue that human activities that emit greenhouse gases are causing at least some climate change. Is this appeal to authority a strong argument? To assess it, we need to ask our questions.

First, did the arguer cite the authority correctly? Some environmentalists fail to cite qualifications in the IPCC reports. This omission might distort their arguments, so we need to check carefully. Still, many passages in their reports do show that the IPCC really does conclude that human emissions are causing some climate change.

Second, can the cited authority be trusted to tell the truth? This question asks whether the scientists in the IPCC have motives to exaggerate the extent of climate change. If so, we have some reason to distrust them. In fact, the members of the IPCC have incentives to uncover mistakes, because their reputations will suffer if they mess up. It would be too far-fetched to imagine a conspiracy among so many disparate scientists.

Third, is the cited authority in fact an authority in the appropriate area? Here we need to check the credentials and areas of expertise of the members of the IPCC. We find that they were chosen because their expertise was relevant.

Fourth, is there agreement among the appropriate experts on this issue? The IPCC does not agree on every issue, and a few dissenters remain outside the mainstream. Nonetheless, the goal of bringing together so many diverse experts in the IPCC is to determine which claims they do agree on and then to get them to sign their joint report on the points of agreement.

Fifth, why is an appeal to authority being made at all? Because the future and causes of climate change are unclear without extensive research and also because proposals to reduce climate change are likely to impose serious costs on many people. This issue matters, so we need to be careful.

After asking these questions, an accurate appeal to the authority of the IPCC ends up looking very good, so we do have strong reasons to believe that climate change is being increased by human activities that emit greenhouse gases. This assessment does not mean that there are no problems in the IPCC. Nothing is perfect. The point is only that this institution is self-correcting, like science as a whole. The IPCC still might be wrong, and future evidence might undermine its claims. That is a risk with all inductive arguments. But inductive arguments can be strong without certainty, so the IPCC reports can give us strong reason to believe that at least some climate change results from human activities.

Nonetheless, this scientific conclusion by itself cannot solve the policy issues regarding what to do about climate change or global warming. The IPCC is often cited as an authority not only on the future and causes of climate change but also on what the government should do about it. To assess this different appeal to authority, we should focus on the question, 'Is the cited authority in fact an authority in the appropriate area?' A negative answer is suggested because climate scientists are experts on science rather than on government policy. A climate scientist who knows that reducing greenhouse gas emissions will slow global warming still might not have the expertise to know whether or how much carbon taxes or the cap-and-trade system will succeed in reducing greenhouse gas emissions, whether or how much these policies will slow economic growth, and whether these policies are politically feasible or would violate standing laws. To settle those separate issues, we need experts from outside of science. Thus our questions can illuminate not only the strengths but also the limits of science.

These questions are not foolproof of course. Opponents will often give very different answers when they ask whether there is agreement among experts and whether a certain source is an authority in the appropriate area and can be trusted to tell the truth. These continuing controversies show that we should not merely ask these questions by ourselves. We should ask other people to ask these questions. We should also not simply ask allies who agree with us. Instead, we should ask our opponents. And we should ask them not only who is an authority to be trusted, but also *why* they trust those authorities. We need to ask for reasons to back up any appeal to authority, at least in controversial areas. This example shows again why we need to learn to ask the right questions, including questions about reasons.

Have we gone anywhere yet?

The third kind of fallacy makes no progress beyond its premises. More technically, an argument *begs the question* when its premises need to be justified but cannot be justified without assuming or depending on its conclusion. This meaning is not far from common parlance, such as 'My blood sugar levels are very high, which begs the question of why I am eating cake.' Here 'begs the question' means 'raises the question'. Similarly, an argument begs the question when it raises the question of why we should believe its premises if we doubt its conclusion.

Here's a common example: 'The death penalty is immoral, because it is always wrong to kill.' The death penalty by definition involves killing, so this argument is valid in our technical sense. It is not possible for its premise to be true when its conclusion is false, because the death penalty must be immoral if all forms of killing are immoral. Despite its validity, this argument fails to justify anything, because there is no way to justify its premise that killing is *always* wrong without already assuming its conclusion that killing is wrong in the particular case of the death penalty. The death penalty might be the one exception that shows why not all killing is wrong, because what is really wrong is killing *innocent* people. Defenders of the argument need to justify its premise without assuming its conclusion, but they have not done that yet in the simple argument as stated, and it is hard to see how they would justify its premise independently of its conclusion.[9] In this way, the argument assumes its conclusion from the start, so it gets nowhere.

The same fallacy can be committed on the other side by arguing like this: 'The death penalty is moral, because we should repay a life for a life.' Again, the premise that we should repay a life for a life already assumes that the death penalty is moral, since the death penalty for murder is repaying a life for a life. Thus this argument cannot justify its conclusion, because its premise needs to be justified and cannot be justified without already assuming its conclusion.

Here's another infamous example: 'The Bible says that God exists. The Bible is the word of God (as it says in II Timothy 3:16). God would not speak words that are not true. Therefore, God truly exists.' The premise that the Bible is the word of God begs the question in two ways. First, a being cannot speak any word without existing, so this premise already assumes the conclusion that God exists. Second, II Timothy 3:16 is part of the Bible, so it also begs the question to cite that verse as evidence that the Bible is the word of God. What argument gives us reason to believe what the Bible says about itself?

The same kind of fallacy is committed by some opponents of religion when they argue like this: 'This evolutionary biologist says that the theory of evolution is true. Evolutionary biologists would not say anything untrue about evolution. Therefore, the theory of evolution is true.' The second premise begs the question because it assumes the conclusion that the theory of evolution is true. If the theory of evolution were not true, then evolutionary biologists would say something untrue about evolution (contrary to premise 2) when they say that the theory of evolution is true (as reported in premise 1). As a result, this simple appeal to evolutionary biologists cannot justify its conclusion any more than the preceding religious appeal to the Bible. Scientists need independent justification for their theories just as much as theologians do. The crucial question is who has such justification.

As always, this criticism of the argument does not imply that the conclusion in any of these pairs of arguments is either true or false. The point, instead, is simply that the issue cannot be resolved with arguments like these, because they beg the question. Some other argument is needed. Whether a better argument is possible will be controversial, but it is significant progress to recognize which arguments fail.

Is that all?

Have we covered all of the fallacies that people ever commit? Of course not. There are plenty more. Some fall into patterns like those we discussed. Genetic fallacies, appeals to ignorance and *tu quoque* (or appeal to hypocrisy) resemble ad hominem arguments. Appeals to emotion, to personal experience, to tradition and to popular opinion resemble appeals to authority. False dichotomy sometimes resembles begging the question. These other arguments can be understood by comparing them to the fallacies that they resemble. Still other fallacies form new patterns, such as the gambler's fallacy, fallacies of composition and division, false cause and so on. Some books and websites list hundreds of fallacies.[10] We will not do that here. Long lists are boring.

So-called fallacies on standard lists are not always fallacious. We saw that slippery-slope arguments and appeals to authority sometimes provide strong reasons. This potential makes it misleading to refer to the general type of argument simply as a fallacy.

The same point applies to appeals to emotion, which are often seen as fallacious and opposed to reason. When someone describes the anguish and weariness of refugees as well as their empathy for refugees and revulsion at the ways they are treated, these emotions can provide good reasons to help refugees, because the emotions point to suffering and injustice. These emotions show nothing if they are irrational, but normal emotions can sometimes be reliable guides, much like authorities. We can decide when to trust emotions by asking questions much like those we asked about appeals to authority. Why am I feeling this emotion now? Are my emotions distorted by self-interest or irrelevant motives? Do other people feel this same emotion in similar situations? Does this emotion reliably react to relevant facts in the world (such as suffering and injustice)? We need to be careful when we appeal to emotions, just as we need to be careful when we appeal to authorities, but some appeals to emotion are not fallacious.

More generally, we should not be too quick to accuse opponents of fallacies. They do not commit an ad hominem fallacy every time they criticize a person. They do not commit a slippery-slope fallacy every time they use a word that is slightly imprecise (like all words). They do not commit a fallacy of appealing to tradition every time they point out that their views align with tradition. When accusations of fallacy become a knee-jerk reaction without thought, they cease to be illuminating and become annoying and polarizing. Such name-calling is not much better than simply announcing, 'I disagree.'

Instead of abusing opponents with names of fallacies, we need to look carefully and charitably at each argument. In particular, we should always ask whether what appears to be a fallacy can be fixed simply by adding a suppressed premise. For example, suppose someone argues that a government employee did not reveal classified information on her private server, because we cannot find any specific email on that server that revealed anything classified. Or suppose someone argues that a political candidate did not collude with the enemy, because we cannot prove that he did. In both cases, critics could retort, 'Appeal to ignorance! That's a fallacy!'

That label will not help anyone understand the issues. It would be much more constructive to ask whether the argument assumes a suppressed premise. It does: 'If he or she had done it, we would know (or at least have the kind of evidence that we lack).' That suppressed premise is true in some cases: if my son had wrecked my car last night, I would probably see dents in my car. But that same suppressed premise is false in other cases: if my son has come home late, I would know (even though I was sound asleep). In every case of appeal to ignorance, then, we need to ask whether the suppressed premise is true: if an email did reveal classified information, would we find it? If the candidate did collude, would we know it? In order to get beyond name-calling and figure out how strong an argument really is, we need to reconstruct the argument as charitably as possible and then ask how strong it is in its best form.

Of course, some arguments will still end up fallacious. We should not be too quick to accuse, but we should also not be too slow to point out fallacies and weaknesses in arguments. Moreover, we need to be able to find and explain flaws in arguments even when we do not have a name for those flaws. The next chapter will teach that skill.

CHAPTER 11

How to Refute Arguments

Many people talk as if all you need to do in order to refute a position is simply to deny it or say anything at all in reply to it. Such talk is too loose. Monty Python taught that 'argument is not just contradiction' or denial. Even if you go beyond denial and say something in reply, not every response is a refutation.

For example, suppose a theist argues, 'God exists, because nothing else could explain the existence of the Universe.' An atheist cannot refute that argument simply by saying 'No, God does not exist' or 'I do not believe in God' or 'That's stupid.' The same goes for the other side. If an atheist argues, 'Evil exists, so God does not', a theist cannot refute that argument simply by saying 'God does exist' or 'I believe in God' or 'That's silly.' These simple responses are not refutations.

In order to refute an argument, you need to give an adequate reason to doubt that argument. We saw that some arguments give reasons that justify belief in their conclusions, whereas other arguments give reasons that explain phenomena. In contrast, refutations give reasons to doubt other arguments. Thus refutation is a new purpose of arguments in addition to justification and explanation.

The reasons supplied by refutations are reasons to doubt

rather than reasons to believe. In order to refute a theist's argument that God exists, atheists do not have to show that God does *not* exist. All atheists need is an adequate reason to doubt that the theist's argument provides enough reason to believe that God does exist. Similarly, theists can refute an atheist's argument against God's existence without giving any reason to believe that God does exist. All the theist needs is an adequate reason to doubt that the atheist's argument shows that God does not exist. Refutation can lead to doubt and suspension of belief in both directions.

Many people who refute arguments do go on to deny those arguments' conclusions. That additional move results in part from the discomfort of admitting, 'I don't know.' Many atheists who refute arguments for God's existence conclude that God does not exist, partly because they do not want to end up as a wishy-washy agnostic. For similar reasons, many theists who refute arguments against God's existence jump to the conclusion that God exists. That additional claim does not, however, follow from the refutation alone. All that the refutation by itself supports is doubt, not belief.

What does it mean to doubt an argument? It means simply to doubt that the argument gives enough reason to believe its conclusion. This doubt can be directed at different parts of the argument. According to our definition of arguments, an argument includes premises and a conclusion and presents the premises as a reason for the conclusion, so a refutation has three main targets to aim at. First, refutations can give reasons to doubt one or more premises. Second, refutations can give reasons to doubt the conclusion. Third, refutations can give reasons to doubt that the premises provide adequate support for the conclusion. We will survey these forms of refutation in turn.

Does the exception prove the rule?

The first way to refute an argument is to cast doubt on its premises. This task can be accomplished either by giving some reason to believe that the premise is not true or by finding some fallacy in the strongest argument for that premise. We will focus here on one common method of refuting premises, namely providing counter-examples.

Suppose that a business owner argues, 'Higher taxes always reduce employment, so we need to keep taxes low.' One way to raise doubts about this argument is to give a reason to doubt or deny its premise that higher taxes always reduce employment. That's easy. Just point to one time when taxes went up to a high level without employment going down. That one counter-example is enough to show that higher taxes do not *always* reduce employment.

But is this refutation strong? Not if the opponent has an easy reply. To respond, all the arguer needs is a guarding term: 'Fine, so high taxes do not always reduce employment. Still, they *usually* do – *almost* always.' A single counter-example cannot raise doubts about this guarded premise. The arguer can claim that this counter-example is the exception that proves the rule in the sense that its exceptional features show that the rule holds in normal cases (rather than in the original sense of this slogan, which was that the exception tests the rule).

That response is not the end of the discussion, however.

As soon as the arguer admits an exception, it raises the question of whether the case under discussion is more like the rule or more like the exception. If we are trying to determine whether 'we need to keep taxes low' (as the conclusion claims), then we need to figure out whether our current circumstances are more like the exceptional period when taxes go up and employment does not go down, or more like the usual periods when taxes go up and employment does go down. It is not enough to give a single counter-example and then stop thinking. That further issue will not be easy to settle, but it should not be ignored.

The same goes for every counter-example. Many religious and cultural traditions espouse something like the golden rule: 'Do unto others as you would have them do unto you' (Matthew 7:12). It is easy to think up counter-examples to this esteemed principle. It is not wrong for judges to sentence murderers to prison, even though the judges would want not to be sentenced to prison themselves. It is not right for sadomasochists to whip their victims, even if they would like to be whipped themselves.

Examples like these raise doubts about the golden rule, but how could its defenders respond? The obvious point about sadomasochists is that their (non-masochistic) victims do not consent to being whipped, whereas sadomasochists would like being whipped only in ways and at times to which they consent. Thus the golden rule still holds if we apply it only to the act of whipping without consent. Nobody likes to be the victim of that.

In the other counter-example, the judge would not like to be sentenced to prison even if she deserved it because she was guilty of a crime. However, the judge would presumably admit that punishing her would be fair in those circumstances. If so, then we can avoid this counter-example by reformulating the golden rule like this: 'Do to others as it would be fair for them to do to you.' What is wrong is then determined by what is fair instead of what you happen to like. The problem is that this reformulation of the golden rule cannot be applied to cases without determining in advance what is fair in those cases. That makes it hard to see how this rule could function as a basic principle of morality.

When a counter-example casts doubt on a premise that an argument depends on, the counter-example raises doubts about whether the argument provides adequate reason for its conclusion. After all, if the premise is false, the argument fails. That is how counter-examples to premises can refute arguments. Nonetheless, the conclusion could still be true. Moreover, the argument still might succeed if it can be reformulated in a way that avoids the counter-example and still provides a strong enough reason for the conclusion. Thus, this form of refutation, like all others, is inconclusive. It moves the discussion forward instead of ending it.

Is this absurdity made of straw?

The second way to refute an argument is to cast doubt on its conclusion. If a refutation shows that a conclusion is false, then there must be something wrong with the argument for that conclusion. At least it cannot be sound. This kind of refutation might not reveal specifically what is wrong with the argument, but it can still show that something went wrong somewhere in the argument. We know that we took a wrong turn somewhere if we end up in a ditch.

The strongest refutations of this flavour are *reductio ad absurdum* – they reduce the conclusion to absurdity. The clearest absurdities are outright contradictions. If someone gives reasons to believe that China has the largest number of citizens, an opponent could reply: 'That's absurd. Just wait a minute, and it will have more. If China had one more citizen, then it would have an even larger number of citizens, so the number that it used to have cannot be the largest number.' It is contradictory to claim that any number is the largest number.

This *reductio ad absurdum* obviously rests on a misinterpretation. What the arguer meant was not that the number of citizens in China is the largest of all numbers, but only that China has a larger number of citizens than any other country. When a refutation misinterprets a claim in order to make it look absurd (although it is not really absurd when interpreted correctly), the argument attacks a straw man or a straw person. The best response to this trick is simply, 'That's not what I meant.'

Real cases are usually subtler. In June 2017, a member of the Israeli parliament pushed for a bill that would have required all professors to give equal time to any position that any student wanted to be discussed. The goal was to enable conservative students to require their liberal professors to consider the conservative side of controversial issues so that students would not be brainwashed towards liberalism. That goal might seem reasonable, but the law would quickly lead to absurdity.

Just imagine a course on neuroscience, whose professor emphasizes the role of the hippocampus in memory. One student says that memory might instead be lodged in the temporal pole. Another suggests that it could be the cingulated cortex. A third suggests the striatum. And so on for every part of the brain. The proposed law requires the professor to give equal time to all of these possibilities. That would be absurd for two reasons. First, there is little evidence linking memory to those other parts of the brain, so what is the professor supposed to discuss? Second, it would take every minute of every class to discuss all of these possibilities, so the course could never proceed to other topics in neuroscience. These absurdities can be cited to refute anyone who argues, 'Every student opinion deserves equal consideration, so professors should give equal time to any position that any student wants to discuss.'

Does this refutation attack a straw man? That is not clear. On the one hand, the proponents of the law were probably thinking of positions in politics rather than neuroscience. If so, these advocates might be able to avoid absurdity by restricting the law to political issues somehow. On the other hand, it is not always clear which issues are political, so proponents of the law might have meant to include debates about politically controversial positions in history and science, such as global warming, the origins of life and the Earth, the efficacy of torture, the causes of certain wars and so on. If the law covered all of these issues as well, then any student could stop professors from discussing any of them simply by advocating an endless number of alternative views with nothing to recommend them (except the student's desire to avoid an impending test). That threat shows that the law would effectively prevent professors from discussing any topic within its scope. Is that absurd? I think so, but maybe that's just because I am a professor. If that result is what proponents of the law want, then they might not see it as absurd.

One lesson from this example is that absurdity is sometimes in the eye of the beholder. Not so in the case of outright contradiction, but often in real cases. Does that mean that *reductios* cannot refute any real arguments? No, but it does reveal that those refutations will work only for limited audiences. This refutation cannot work against extremists who hold that professors should not be able to discuss any controversial issues. Nonetheless, it can still work for moderates who think that professors should be able to discuss the main alternative positions on a controversial issue without spending equal time on every possibility that any student might like to bring up for whatever reason. This case reinforces my earlier point that arguments will never satisfy anyone whose standards are too high, such as those who seek certainty, but they can still be very useful for people with reasonable goals, such as justifying their conclusion to reasonable moderates with open minds.

What is 'just like arguing...'?

The third way to refute an argument is to give reasons to doubt that its premises provide adequate support for its conclusion. This variety of refutation targets defects in the relationship between premises and conclusion rather than in the premises or conclusion themselves.

We saw examples in our discussion of fallacies. Equivocation occurs when a word has a different meaning in the conclusion than it had in a premise. Ad hominem arguments and appeals to authority use premises about believers to support conclusions about their beliefs. And arguments beg the question when their premises are not independent of their conclusions – that is, when premises and conclusion are too closely related.

The relation between premises and conclusion can also be defective in other arguments that do not fit the patterns of standard fallacies. How can we tell whether that relation is defective? The most direct method is to look closely at the argument itself and assess it for validity (if it is deductive) or for strength (if it is inductive). Recall that inductive strength is the conditional probability of the conclusion given the premises. That probability is often hard to calculate or even estimate, so this method has its limits.

Another method is less direct, but sometimes easier to apply. Try to construct a *parallel* argument that mirrors the form of the argument being assessed and has obviously true premises and an obviously false conclusion. If opponents admit that the premises are true and the conclusion is false, then this parallel argument can reveal something defective in the relation between the premises and conclusion in the original argument being assessed. In other words, when someone presents an argument, critics respond, 'That's just like arguing in this parallel way' where the parallel argument has an obvious defect. The original argument can then be defended only by showing that it does not share the same defect.

Martin Luther King deployed this strategy in his 'Letter from Birmingham Jail'. He had been jailed for marching in favour of racial equality and civil rights. His jailers and critics argued that he should not have marched, because this protest would inspire his opponents to violently attack him and other marchers. King replied, 'In your statement you asserted that our actions, even though peaceful, must be condemned because they precipitate violence. But can this assertion be logically made? Isn't this like condemning the robbed man because his possession of money precipitated the evil act of robbery?' In this case, King's critics argued, 'The marchers precipitate violence, so they must be condemned.' He replied, in our terms, 'That's just like arguing that the robbery victim's possession of money precipitated robbery, so the robbery victim must be condemned.'

Pretty powerful reply, right? But what is going on? King does not deny the truth of the premise that the marchers precipitate violence. They do. King also does not argue that the conclusion is false. That could not be shown by switching the subject to robbery. Indeed, King's reply might seem irrelevant. How could talking about robbery show anything about marches? The key lies in the form of the arguments. Because they share a similar form, if one is defective in its form, so is the other. The parallel argument about robbery is supposed to move from a true premise that the robbery victim's acquisition of money precipitated robbery to a false conclusion that this victim should be condemned. That movement shows that there must be some defect in the relation between premises and conclusion in the argument about robbery. If the argument about marches has the same form and the same relation between its premises and its conclusion, then the relation between premises and conclusion in the argument about marches must also be defective.

This reply does not attempt to show that the conclusion of the argument about marches is false. It still might be true that the marchers ought to be condemned. All King has shown is that this one argument is not enough to support that conclusion. He casts doubt on one argument without arguing for the opposite. Moreover, he casts only some doubt. He does not prove beyond any question that the argument fails. His critics still have several moves available.

First, King's critics can accept the conclusion that the robbery victim should be condemned. If that conclusion is true, then the parallel argument is not obviously defective, so this refutation fails to reveal a defect in the original argument. But this reply seems implausible in this case.

Second, King's critics can deny the premise that the robbery victim's possession of money precipitated the robbery. If the robbed person hid his money, as most people do, then the robber would not know whether he had money, so he would have robbed this victim even if he had had no money with him. Since possessing money is not necessary for him to be robbed, his possession of money might not be what causes or precipitates the robbery. This reply is perhaps more plausible, but still problematic.

Third, King's critics can point out differences between the supposedly parallel arguments. The robbery victim did not know that he would be robbed, but King did know that his opponents would attack violently. The robbery victim presumably hid his possessions to avoid robbery, whereas King marched in the open and hid nothing. He wanted publicity.

King cannot deny these differences between the supposedly parallel arguments, but he could deny that these differences make a difference. One way to test what makes a difference is to add premises to each argument. King's critics could reply, 'Fine, we spoke too quickly. But our main point still holds: the marchers knowingly and publicly precipitate violence, so they must be condemned.' To refute this revised argument, King would need to say, 'That's just like arguing that the robbery victim's possession of money knowingly and publicly precipitated robbery, so the robbery victim must be condemned.' The problem is that this new premise is clearly false, so this new argument does not move from true premises to a false conclusion. As a result, it cannot reveal anything defective in the relation between this premise and this conclusion.

As always, the discussion can continue. The point here is only that an attempt to refute an argument by saying 'That's just like arguing . . .' works only if the supposedly parallel argument has true premises and a false conclusion and only if the argument really is parallel. All of that needs to be shown in order for the refutation to work. It is not enough to say, 'That's just like arguing . . .' unless it really is *like* arguing . . .

When this method of refutation is applied properly, it can be used to uncover many kinds of fallacies. Here are a few examples with varying degrees of strength:

THE FALLACY OF COMPOSITION

Argument: If one person doubles her income, then she will be better off.

Therefore, if all people double their incomes, then they will all be better off.

Refutation: That's like arguing that if I stand up at a concert, then I will see better; so if the entire audience stands up at a concert, then they will all see better.

Lesson: What holds for parts might not hold for the whole.

THE FALLACY OF DIVISION

Argument: North Korea is an aggressive country, and you are from North Korea, so you must be aggressive.

Refutation: That's like arguing that North Korea is a mountainous country, and you are from North Korea, so you must be mountainous.

Lesson: What holds for the whole might not hold for parts.

FALSE DICHOTOMY

Argument: You are either with us or against us, and you are not yet fully committed to our cause, so you must be our enemy.

Refutation: That's like arguing that you are either with Fiji or against Fiji, and you are not yet fully committed to Fiji, so you must be an enemy of Fiji.

Lesson: People can be neutral – neither for nor against.

FALSE EQUIVALENCE

Argument: There is some argument for adopting this policy, but there is also some argument against it and in favour of an alternative; so both sides are reasonable, and it is unreasonable to favour one over the other.

Refutation: That's like arguing that there is some argument for jumping off this building (how thrilling!), and there is also some argument against jumping off (how deadly!); so both choices are reasonable, and it is unreasonable to favour one over the other.

Lesson: Not all arguments and reasons are equivalent. Some are better than others. (The same point holds when there are experts on both sides.)

APPEAL TO IGNORANCE

Argument: You can't prove that there were weapons of mass destruction in Iraq, so there must have been none.

Refutation: That's like arguing that you can't prove that there are tiny spiders in this room, so there must not be any tiny spiders in this room.

Lesson: There might have been lots that we did not see, because they are hard to find, even when they are there.

FALSE CAUSE (OR *POST HOC ERGO PROPTER HOC*)

Argument: Our economy improved right after he became President, so he helped our country a lot.

Refutation: That's like arguing that our economy improved right after my daughter was born, so she helped our country a lot.

Lesson: The timing might be a coincidence. More generally, correlation does not imply causation.

None of these refutations is conclusive. In each case, defenders of the argument could claim that (a) the premise in the refutation is false; (b) the conclusion in the refutation is true; or (c) the argument in the refutation is not really parallel to the original argument, because they differ in some relevant respect.

Such attempts at refutation still shift the burden of proof to the defender of the argument, so even inconclusive refutations can make progress. They do not end the discussion, but that is not their purpose. Their goal is to rule out simple mistakes, and they can do that. When arguers succeed in defending their arguments against refutations by parallel reasoning, they usually need to complicate their arguments and add qualifications. The refutation shows that the original argument without the qualifications oversimplified the issues. The revised argument reveals complexities and subtleties that the original overlooked. Refutation can thereby improve discussions without ending them.

Rules to Live By

Now you know something about why we need arguments, what arguments are, how to analyse them, how to evaluate them and how to recognize fallacies. What next?

First, admit your limits. This short book has barely scratched the surface. You have seen some purposes of arguments, some words in arguments, some valid forms of argument, some kinds of induction and some fallacies. That is a lot to have covered, but please do not imagine that you know it all. Nobody does.

Second, learn more. To understand arguments and reasons fully will take a lifetime. In addition to exploring further kinds of arguments,[1] we all need to know more about language (our shared means of communication), science (including psychology and economics), mathematics (especially statistics and probability), and philosophy (which explores our basic assumptions and values). There is much more to study.

Third, keep practising. The only effective way to learn how to identify, analyse, evaluate and avoid fallacies in arguments and reasons is to practise, practise and practise again. The best way to practise is with other people, and the best people to practise with are people who disagree with you, but sincerely want to understand you and to be understood by you. If you can find such partners, you are lucky. Treasure them and use them.

Fourth, construct your own arguments. When you want to think about an important issue, construct the best argument that you can on both sides of that issue. (For example, if you want to decide whether to buy a larger car or a smaller car, spell out the reasons on both sides, such as greater comfort in a larger car, and less environmental impact from a smaller car. And if you can vote in an election, specify the reasons for and against each candidate, such as more focus on issues that matter to you or less ability to get anything done.) After setting out your reasons in discursive form, do a close analysis and a deep analysis of your own argument and evaluate its validity and strength. If you do this honestly, you will gain a better understanding of your beliefs, your values and yourself. Then ask a friend, colleague or opponent to analyse and evaluate your arguments, and return the favour. This exchange will help you both understand each other better.

Fifth, use your skills – throughout your daily life, including internet chats, political debates and other contexts where polarization and incivility run rampant. Don't simply declare what you believe: offer arguments. Don't let others merely announce their positions: ask questions about their reasons. Don't interrupt: listen carefully to their answers. Don't attack opponents too soon: interpret them charitably. Don't insult or abuse opponents: be civil and respectful. Don't commit fallacies: be critical of your own reasoning. Don't think that you have all the answers: be humble.

Sixth, teach others. The skills that you have learned are not widely enough shared, so share them as much as you can. One method involves explicit training or lengthy discussions about argumentation, but that is not the only way. You can also teach others simply by pointing out problems as they arise in informal contexts. When one person interrupts another, you can ask, 'What were you saying before you were interrupted?' When someone calls an opponent crazy or stupid, you can say, 'I don't think you are crazy. I want to understand your point of view.' When a speaker presents a bad argument, you can specify precisely what is bad about it. When they present a good argument, you can say why it is good. We too often let teaching opportunities like these slip by.

We cannot always follow these rules. It takes too long to practise or to construct and listen to arguments on every issue. Nobody has that much patience or time. Moreover, not every circumstance is right for teaching, and not every audience is amenable to learning. Even incivility is sometimes justified. Nonetheless, we could all benefit from following these rules more than we do now. So let's get started.

Notes

CHAPTER 1: SO CLOSE AND YET SO FAR

1. Nathaniel Persily, 'Introduction', in Nathaniel Persily (ed.), *Solutions to Political Polarization in America* (New York: Cambridge University Press, 2015), p. 4. My discussion of kinds of polarization owes a great deal to Persily's insightful introduction. Polarization is sometimes seen as a process instead of a state, but I will discuss polarization as a state.

2. The following statistics come from Pew Research Center, 'Political Polarization in the American Public' (Washington, DC: Pew Research Center, June 2014).

3. Morris P. Fiorina, Samuel J. Adams, and Jeremy Pope, *Culture War? Myth of a Polarized America* (London: Pearson Education, 2005) suggest that these increases in polarization can be explained by 'party sorting'. In reply, Michael J. Barber and Nolan McCarty, 'Causes and Consequences of Polarization', in Persily (ed.), *Solutions to Political Polarization in America*, argue that 'position switching is more common than party switching' (p. 22). Polarization between parties still does not prove that Americans as a whole have grown more polarized, since moderates might have left both parties to become independents. Polarization between the parties remains a problem in any case.

4. See citations in Linda J. Skitka and Anthony N. Washburn, 'Are Conservatives from Mars and Liberals from Venus? Maybe Not So Much', in Piercarlo Valdesolo and Jesse Graham (eds), *Social Psychology of Political Polarization* (New York and Abingdon: Routledge, 2016), pp. 78–101 at p. 94–5. There is an active debate on whether liberals are more likely than conservatives to reject the science of GMOs, vaccines and nuclear waste, but there is no doubt that many liberals go against the scientific consensus on these issues.

5. Donald Braman, Dan M. Kahan, Ellen Peters, Maggie Wittlin, Paul Slovic, Lisa Larrimore Ouellette and Gregory N. Mandel, 'The Polarizing Impact of Science Literacy and Numeracy on Perceived Climate Change Risks', *Nature Climate Change*, 2 (2012), 732.

6. Barber and McCarty, 'Causes and Consequences of Polarization', p. 38.

7. David R. Mayhew, *Divided We Govern: Party Control, Lawmaking, and Investigations*, 1946–2002 (New Haven: Yale University Press, 2005).

8. The statistics in this section come from Pew Research Center, Washington, DC, 'Political Polarization in the American Public' in 2014 and 2016.

9. Shanto Iyengar, Gaurav Sood and Yphtach Lelkes, 'Affect, Not Ideology: A Social Identity Perspective on Polarization', *Public Opinion Quarterly* 76 (3) (2012), 405.

10. Pew Research Center, 'Political Polarization in the American Public' (2014).

11. Jonathan Rodden, 'Geography and Gridlock in the United States', in Persily (ed.), *Solutions to Political Polarization in America*, p. 118.

12. Rodden, 'Geography and Gridlock in the United States', p. 117.

13. See Roshini Wickremesinhe and Sanjana Hattotuwa, 'Voting in Hate: A Study of Hate Speech on Facebook Surrounding Sri Lanka's Parliamentary Election of 2015', Centre for Policy Alternatives, Colombo, Sri Lanka (March 2016), at <http://www.cpalanka.org/wp-content/uploads/2016/03/Voting-in-Hate-1.pdf>

14. See Thitinan Pongsudhirak, 'Thai Voters in Yellow and Red Set for Crucial Elections', *The Korea Herald*, 21 March 2011, at <http://www.koreaherald.com/view.php?ud=20110321000145>

15. See Hyunji Lee, 'Polarized Electorates in South Korea and Taiwan: The Role of Political Trust under Conservative Governments', at <https://fsi.stanford.edu/sites/default/files/lee_hyunji.oct12_2014.pdf>

16. Hulda Thórisdóttir, 'The Left–Right Landscape Over Time: The View from a Western European Multi-Party Democracy', in Valdesolo and Graham (eds), *Social Psychology of Political Polarization*, pp. 38–58 at p. 42.

17. Thórisdóttir, 'The Left–Right Landscape Over Time: The View from a Western European Multi-Party Democracy', p. 42.

18. Thórisdóttir, 'The Left–Right Landscape Over Time: The View from a Western European Multi-Party Democracy', p. 46.

CHAPTER 2: TOXIC TALK

1. Discussed by Daniel C. Dennett, *Intuition Pumps and Other Tools for Thinking* (New York: W. W. Norton, 2013), pp. 31–5.

2. See Ben Shapiro, 'The Left Loses its Damn Mind', *The Ben Shapiro Show*, Episode 140, at <https://soundcloud.com/benshapiroshow/ep140>

3. See Boris Johnson, 'Boris Johnson's Speech on the EU Referendum: Full Text', 9 May 2016, at <http://www.conservativehome.com/parliament/2016/05/boris-johnsons-speech-on-the-eu-referendum-full-text.html>

4. See tweet by Sayeeda Warsi, 'Toxic, divisive & xenophobic political campaigning should have no place in a liberal democracy', 20 June 2016, at <https://twitter.com/SayeedaWarsi/status/744787830333804544>. Compare tweet by Angela Merkel, 'Hatred, racism, and extremism have no place in this country', 5 May 2017.

5. See J. K. Rowling, 'On Monsters, Villains and the EU Referendum', 30 June 2016, at <https://www.jkrowling.com/opinions/monsters-villains-eu-referendum/>

6. See Arun Kundnani, 'The Right-Wing Populism That Drove Brexit Can Only be Fought With a Genuinely Radical Alternative', *AlterNet*, 2 July 2016, at <http://www.alternet.org/world/right-wing-populism-drove-brexit-can-only-be-fought-genuinely-radical-alternative>

7. See Sandy Marrero, 'When it Comes to Human Dignity, We Cannot Make Compromises', *Prezi*, 3 January 2015, at < https://prezi.com/lfqwky4jv6em/when-it-comes-to-human-dignity-we-cannot-make-compromises/>

8. See Sarah Wildman, 'Marine Le Pen is Trying to Win the French Elections with a Subtler Kind of Xenophobia', *Vox*, 6 May 2017, at <https://www.vox.com/world/2017/4/21/15358708/marine-le-pen-french-elections-far-right-front-national>

9. Diana Mutz, *In-Your-Face Politics: The Consequences of Uncivil Media* (Princeton, NJ: Princeton University Press, 2015), Chapter 2.

10. Cass R. Sunstein, *#Republic: Divided Democracy in the Age of Social Media* (Princeton, NJ: Princeton University Press, 2017), p. 86.

11. Mutz, *In-Your-Face Politics: The Consequences of Uncivil Media*, Chapter 3.

CHAPTER 3: THE SOUND OF SILENCING

1. 'Partisanship and Political Animosity in 2016: Highly Negative Views of the Opposing Party and its Members' (Washington, DC: Pew Research Center,

22 June 2016), p. 2, at <http://www.people-press.org/2016/06/22/partisanship-and-political-animosity-in-2016/>

2. For example, Elisabeth Noelle-Neumann, *The Spiral of Silence: Public Opinion – Our Social Skin* (Chicago, IL: University of Chicago Press, 1984).

3. Cf. Miranda Fricker, *Epistemic Injustice: Power and the Ethics of Knowing* (Oxford: Oxford University Press, 2007).

4. Gregory J. Martin and Ali Yurukoglu, 'Bias in Cable News: Persuasion and Polarization', Working Paper #20798 (Cambridge, MA: National Bureau of Economic Research, December 2014).

5. See Jeffrey Gottfried and Elisa Shearer, 'News Use Across Social Media Platforms 2016', Pew Research Center: Journalism & Media, 26 May 2016, at <http://www.journalism.org/2016/05/26/news-use-across-social-media-platforms-2016/>

6. For an interesting example, see <https://www.buzzfeed.com/lamvo/facebook-filter-bubbles-liberal-daughter-conservative-mom>

7. *Obergefell v. Hodges*, 576 U.S.___ (2015). On another issue, a Pew Research Center survey in 2012 found that 76 per cent of respondents expressed an opinion about the Supreme Court ruling on the Affordable Care Act, but only 55 per cent responded correctly when asked what the Supreme Court had decided.

8. Cengiz Erisen, Dave Redlawsk and Elif Erisen, 'Complex Thinking as a Result of Incongruent Information Exposure', *American Politics Research* (30 August 2017); DOI: 10.1177/1532673X17725864.

9. Cass R. Sunstein, *#Republic: Divided Democracy in the Age of Social Media* (Princeton, NJ: Princeton University Press, 2017), pp. 91–2.

10. James S. Fishkin, *The Voice of the People: Public Opinion and Democracy* (New Haven, CT: Yale University Press, 1995). But cf. also Ian Shapiro, 'Collusion in Restraint of Democracy: Against Political Deliberation', *Daedalus*, 146 (3) (Summer 2017), 77–84.

11. This website can be found at <https://www.reddit.com/r/changemyview/>. See also Sunstein, *#Republic*, pp. 134, note 69 and 232, note 20.

CHAPTER 4: WHAT ARGUMENTS CAN DO

1. David Hume, *A Treatise of Human Nature* (1738), II.3.3, 415.

2. David Hume, *An Enquiry Concerning the Principles of Morals* (1751), Section 1, paragraph 9.

3. See 'Migrant Crisis: Migrant Europe Explained in Seven Charts', 4 March 2016, at <http://www.bbc.com/news/world-europe-34131911>

4. Dale Carnegie, *How to Win Friends and Influence People* (New York: Simon & Schuster, 1936).

5. Oscar Wilde, *The Happy Prince and Other Stories* (London, 1888).

6. See Megan Phelps-Roper, 'I Grew Up in the Westboro Baptist Church. Here's Why I Left', March 2017, at <https://www.ted.com/talks/megan_phelps_roper_i_grew_up_in_the_westboro_baptist_church_here_s_why_i_left/transcript?language=en>. See also Adrian Chen, 'Unfollow: How a Prized Daughter of Westboro Baptist Church Came to Question its Beliefs', *The New Yorker*, 23 November 2015. More examples of radical conversion in light of evidence can be found in *The Best of Enemies: Race and Redemption in the New South* by Osha Gray Davidson (New York: Scribner's, 1996) about civil rights activist Ann Atwater and former Ku Klux Klan leader C. P. Ellis; in Matthew Ornstein's documentary *Accidental Courtesy: Daryl Davis, Race & America* (2016) on Netflix about a black musician who befriended Ku Klux Klan members; and in stories about Derek Black, former white nationalist.

7. P. M. Fernbach, T. Rogers, C. R. Fox and S. A. Sloman, 'Political Extremism is Supported by an Illusion of Understanding', *Psychological Science*, 24 (6) (2013), 939–46. In their later book, *The Knowledge Illusion: Why We Never Think Alone* (London: Macmillan, 2017), Chapter 9, Sloman and Fernbach add two important qualifications. First, *how*-questions have different effects with regard to sacred values (such as abortion) compared to policy issues (such as cap and trade). Second, *how*-questions that expose people's illusions and ignorance can also upset some people and make them less inclined to discuss the issue. Like all tools, questions work only in some contexts and need to be used carefully and sparingly.

8. Among their other works on accountability, see Jennifer S. Lerner, Julie H. Goldberg and Philip E. Tetlock, 'Sober Second Thought: The Effects of Accountability, Anger, and Authoritarianism on Attributions of Responsibility', *Personality and Social Psychology Bulletin*, 24 (6) (1998), 563–74.

9. Jaime Napier and Jamie Luguri, 'From Silos to Synergies: The Effects of Construal Level on Political Polarization', in Piercarlo Valdesolo and Jesse Graham (eds), *Social Psychology of Political Polarization* (New York and Abingdon: Routledge, 2016), pp. 143–61.

10. Pew Research Center, Washington, DC, 'Political Polarization in the American Public' (June 2014), p. 59.

11. As they are called by Avishai Margalit, *On Compromise and Rotten Compromises* (Princeton, NJ: Princeton University Press, 2009).

CHAPTER 5: WHY LEARN HOW TO ARGUE?

1. Marilyn vos Savant, 'Ask Marilyn', *Parade* magazine (1990).
2. This mistake is one instance of a more general pattern discussed in Daniel C. Molden and E. Tory Higgins, 'Motivated Thinking', in Keith J. Holyoak and Robert G. Morrison (eds), *The Cambridge Handbook of Thinking and Reasoning* (New York: Cambridge University Press, 2005), pp. 295–317.
3. Ben M. Tappin, Leslie van der Leer and Ryan T. McKay, 'The Heart Trumps the Head: Desirability Bias in Political Belief Revision', *Journal of Experimental Psychology: General*, 146 (8) (August 2017), 1143–9.
4. Daniel Kahneman, Paul Slovic and Amos Tversky (eds), *Judgment Under Uncertainty: Heuristics and Biases* (Cambridge: Cambridge University Press, 1982), Chapter 4. A better-known example of the representativeness heuristic is Linda, the feminist bank teller (Chapter 6).
5. Leda Cosmides and John Tooby, 'Can a General Deontic Logic Capture the Facts of Human Moral Reasoning? How the Mind Interprets Social Exchange Rules and Detects Cheaters', in Walter Sinnott-Armstrong (ed.), *Moral Psychology*, Volume 1: *The Evolution of Morality: Adaptations and Innateness* (Cambridge, MA: MIT Press, 2007), pp. 53–120.
6. Hugo Mercier and Dan Sperber, 'Why Do Humans Reason? Arguments for an Argumentative Theory', *Behavioral and Brain Sciences* 34 (2) (2011), 57–111 at 63 and 72. See also Hugo Mercier and Dan Sperber, *The Enigma of Reason* (Cambridge, MA: Harvard University Press, 2017).
7. This process of correction in science is described by Miriam Solomon, *Social Empiricism* (Cambridge, MA: MIT Press, 2007).
8. R. Ritchhart and D. N. Perkins, 'Learning to Think: The Challenges of Teaching Thinking', in Holyoak and Morrison (eds), *The Cambridge Handbook of Thinking and Reasoning*, pp. 775. These negative results could reflect deficiencies in particular teaching methods that were tested.
9. Mercier and Sperber, 'Why Do Humans Reason?', 57–111.

CHAPTER 6: HOW TO SPOT ARGUMENTS

1. See Monty Python, 'Argument Clinic' sketch (1976), at <https://www.youtube.com/watch?v=kQFKtI6gn9Y&t=136s>
2. See below on ad hominem fallacies.
3. This definition comes from Robert Fogelin. He and I have defended a close relative in Walter Sinnott-Armstrong and Robert Fogelin, *Understanding Arguments: An Introduction to Informal Logic*, 9th edn (Stamford, CT: Cengage Advantage Books, 2014).
4. I will not bother with technical issues about whether the premises and conclusion are statements, propositions or sentences, since that nicety does not affect the general issues in this book. I will also allow arguments with a single premise, but they must have at least one premise. What if the speaker knows that the premises are not really reasons at all, but he presents them as such in order to fool some audiences? I am inclined to think that what he gives is an argument, even though he does not intend its premises to be real reasons for its conclusion. This explains why I define arguments as presenting reasons, which means that their premises are intended to be seen as reasons.
5. Aristotle, *Physics*, II, 3, and *Metaphysics*, V, 2. Notice that an arguer's desire for an argument to serve a purpose is what causes the arguer to give the argument.
6. 'Conservative South Koreans Rally against President Park's Impeachment', *Asia Times*, 17 December 2016, at <http://www.atimes.com/article/conservative-south-koreans-rally-parks-impeachment/>

CHAPTER 7: HOW TO STOP ARGUMENTS

1. For hilarious examples, see literallyunbelievable.org and Snopes.com.
2. Sextus Empiricus, *Outlines of Pyrrhonism*.
3. See Walter Sinnott-Armstrong, *Moral Skepticisms* (New York: Oxford University Press, 2006), Chapter 4.
4. For details on how to limit our goals to certain contrast classes, see my *Moral Skepticisms*, Chapter 5.
5. Ludwig Wittgenstein, *On Certainty*, edited by G. E. M. Anscombe and G. H. von Wright (Oxford: Basil Blackwell, 1969).
6. Cass R. Sunstein, Sebastian Bobadilla-Suarez, Stephanie C. Lazzaro and Tali Sharot, 'How People Update Beliefs about Climate Change: Good News

and Bad News' (forthcoming; written 2 September 2016 and available at SSRN: https://ssrn.com/abstract=2821919 or http://dx.doi.org/10.2139/ssrn.2821919).

7. J. O. Urmson, 'On Grading', *Mind*, 59 (234) (1950), 145–69.

8. Advertisement for Equal Exchange fair trade coffee, Copyright © 1997, 1998, 1999.

CHAPTER 8: HOW TO COMPLETE ARGUMENTS

1. Which kind of possibility? Consider 'This building is 100 metres tall, so I cannot jump over it.' Is this argument valid if jumping over 100 metres is conceptually possible but not physically possible? Luckily, such tricky cases will not affect my main points here, so I will not pause to worry about these complications.

2. See Walter Sinnott-Armstrong and Robert Fogelin, *Understanding Arguments: An Introduction to Informal Logic*, 9th edn (Stamford, CT: Cengage Advantage Books, 2014), Chapters 6–7.

3. 'New Approaches Needed to Address Rise of Poor Urban Villages in the Pacific', *Asia Today*, 19 October 2016, at <http://www.asiatoday.com/pressrelease/new-approaches-needed-address-rise-poor-urban-villages-pacific>

CHAPTER 9: HOW TO EVALUATE ARGUMENTS

1. 'The Greek Interpreter', in Sir Arthur Conan Doyle, *The Memoirs of Sherlock Holmes* (London: George Newnes, 1894), p.183.

2. John Dewey, *The Quest for Certainty: A Study of the Relation of Knowledge and Action* (New York: Capricorn, 1960).

3. It might sometimes be more intuitive to think of the strength of inductive arguments in terms of conditional reasons instead of conditional probability. Contrast Keith Lehrer, *Knowledge* (Oxford: Clarendon Press, 1974), which analysed justification in terms of probability, with Keith Lehrer, *Theory of Knowledge* (Routledge, 1990), which analysed justification in terms of reasons. This philosophical distinction will not affect my main points in the text.

4. Assume there are 50,000 cars and 1,000 Fiats in Edinburgh. The witness would identify 90 per cent or 900 of these 1,000 Fiats as Fiats. But he would also misidentify 10 per cent or 4,900 of the 49,000 non-Fiats as Fiats. Thus, out of the 900+4,900=5,800 cars that he would identify as Fiats, only 900/5,800=15.5 per cent really are Fiats.

5. For more on these and other kinds of inductive arguments, see my and Robert Fogelin's textbook, *Understanding Arguments: An Introduction to Informal Logic*, 9th edn (Stamford, CT: Cengage Advantage Books, 2014), and my and Ram Neta's MOOC, 'Think Again: How to Reason and Argue', available on the Coursera website.

6. Martin Luther King, Jr., 'I Have a Dream . . .' speech (1963), at < https://www.archives.gov/files/press/exhibits/dream-speech.pdf>

7. General Colin Powell, Address to the United Nations Security Council, 5 February 2003, at <http://www.americanrhetoric.com/speeches/wariniraq/colinpowellunsecuritycouncil.htm>

CHAPTER 10: HOW TO AVOID FALLACIES

1. From *Squad Helps Dog Bite Victim and Other Flubs from the Nation's Press*, edited by Columbia Journalism Review (Garden City, New York: Doubleday, 1980).

2. From Matthew H. Hurley, Daniel C. Dennett, and Reginald B. Adams, Jr., *Inside Jokes: Using Humor to Reverse-Engineer the Mind* (Cambridge, MA: MIT Press, 2011).

3. Roy Sorensen, 'Vagueness', in Edward N. Zalta (ed.), *The Stanford Encyclopedia of Philosophy* (Winter 2016 edition), at <https://plato.stanford.edu/archives/win2016/entries/vagueness/>

4. 'Torture Memos', Wikipedia, at <https://en.wikipedia.org/wiki/Torture_Memos>

5. Jeffrey Hart, 'Protesters are "Ugly, Stupid"', *King Features*.

6. American Psychological Association. 'Report of the Task Force on the Role of Psychology in the Criminal Justice System', *American Psychologist*, 33 (1978), 1099–1113, at <https://www.ncjrs.gov/App/abstractdb/AbstractDBDetails.aspx?id=62100> This basic point has not changed much since this report.

7. See Miriam Solomon, *Social Empiricism* (Cambridge, MA: MIT Press, 2007).

8. See 'International Panel on Climate Change', Wikipedia, at <https://en.wikipedia.org/wiki/Intergovernmental_Panel_on_Climate_Change>

9. This point might seem to suggest any valid argument from a universal premise begs the question, but it doesn't, as I show in Walter Sinnott-Armstrong, 'Begging the Question', *Australasian Journal of Philosophy*, 77 (2) (1999), 174–91.

10. For example, Gary N. Curtis, 'The Fallacy Files', at <http://www.fallacyfiles.org> and Don Lindsay, 'A List of Fallacious Arguments' (2013), at <http://www.don-lindsay-archive.org/skeptic/arguments.html>

CONCLUSION: RULES TO LIVE BY

1. For more lessons on arguments, see my MOOC with Ram Neta called 'Think Again: How to Reason and Argue' on the Coursera platform and my textbook with Robert Fogelin, *Understanding Arguments: An Introduction to Informal Logic*, 9th edn (Stamford, CT: Cengage Advantage Books, 2014).

Index

PELICAN BOOKS